SCEnES FrOm ThE PLAnET EaRTH

aN aphoriStic meMoir

EduCatiOn & abuSes oF poWer
iN SocioloGical staNzas

tHe reAl prObleM wIt acAdeMia

oR

SomEthiNg oF A nOnLinEar OppOsitioNal
DeFiant PsYcholoGical autoBiograPhy

JOSEPH D. REICH

Sagging
Meniscus

© 2025 by Joseph D. Reich

All Rights Reserved.

Set in Mrs Eaves with LaTeX.

ISBN: 978-1-963846-50-8 (paperback)
Library of Congress Control Number: 2025943871

Sagging Meniscus Press
Montclair, New Jersey
saggingmeniscus.com

Sociological Stanzas
wit a side of sad dire

the wind has blown away the carnival
—joe strummer

Scenes from the Planet Earth

−1

those who play god ironically need jesus in their lives

0

those who play themselves don't do a very good job

01

man has every right to be human . . .
what are the other options & alternatives?

to call back all those phone numbers
on cocktail napkins when you were drunken?

02

why do we always find ourselves vociferously defending
our identity against those who seem to know us the least?

for that rare minority wouldn't a great response be
"i'm innocent! i'm innocent!" but not in the legal

& punitive sense, yet more so the humanistic
the type for some reason who always feel guilty

03

in desperate need to 'make an impression'
what a strange dynamic & expression

similarly, never very much trusted those statements
which started off with such proclamations like 'truth be told'

like those "it's the principle of it all" as one wonders all those
experiences & episodes before ended up calling it a 'principle'

04

"an honest mistake" now there's a linguistic
statement for the ages! an honest mistake—
finding yourself constantly over explaining
to rabble rousers & rapists who never once
say they're sorry or wrong (their stubborness
is what makes them strong) which just makes
you feel so alone in this incongruent, parallel
world full of constant rationalizations coming
from napoleons who make it a very convenient
habit ('convenient amnesia' included) to humbly
histrionically justify their oxymoronic honest mistakes

05

"who you know" far more dangerous
than you may very well think

"think we may know some of the same people"
but do they really at all know themselves?

06

what if life's all just one big magic trick
and all's you need one slight adjustment to
get the whole grand illusion to make sense?

07

I.

in amerika we make determinations on who's the best
& climbs that ladder of success by how they perform
on multiple choice tests like being more sympathetic
to those sadistic idiots in the audience of the coliseum
than the 'sacrifice & slaughter' of that poor stand-in
who's just apparently given up on 'the act' of living

II.

it's my intrinsic belief that the adult of the human species
with their persistent bullshit and lies can waste and wear
you down (and retraumatize) so much so that literally
that cliche holds true 'not sure which way you're coming
or going' forced into that unenviable position of whether to
fight or flee or simply turn to that archetypal stereotypical hero
which seems all but missing-in-action having become some one
dimensional action figure computer-generated spending $10.50
on a movie ticket pouring some sorta cheese whiz all over your
chips washed down with a supersized diet pepsi wondering why
when you leave the theater end up feeling like total shit with no
sense of liberation (or escapism) but moreso experiencing those
instant triggers once again due to some false savior who is just
not believable or convincing with really poor bedside manner

III.

soon the elections are gonna come to amerika again
with that infamous rite of passage—the iowa state fair
where they're gonna prove they're a true man/woman
of the people & become gluttons & stuff their pieholes
with that fried dough or porkchop on a stick or one
of those silly shticks; shake hands & kiss the foreheads
of wailing newborns, seductive lolitas in their tight jeans
seducing both father & son, riding the ferris wheel through
the night round & round & round til find they like it so much
decide to just move out there & never seen from or heard from
again except for some reading light on in the cornfield—that's
who i want for my next president of the united states of amerika

hollywood square or that human cannonball
tumbling down the aisle the next contestant
standing pompous & proud at real-life bully
pulpit for great debate going to instant denial

IV.

i don't know—this country all just seems
like some big fuckin game show of freaks
with its judges all sitting very comfortably
in their big oversized leather seats full of
leftover flabby comedians, rock & rollers,
porn stars, ex-cons & candidates for president
of the united states of amerika (all looking
the same with their pathetic plastic grins) those
contestants who must impress & act submissive
& like the beginning of the hockey season
& end of the political one if only we could just
put those officials in the penalty box; that being
the political ones what a better world we'd live in

Hx:

very brave courageous explorers
show up to the shores of amerika
equipped with their maps & ships
& gps's searching for that infamous
gulf of mexico nowhere to be found
as apparently been renamed by
a strange orange-faced clown
in his blue blazer swinging a
golf club in his self-entitled
resort & country club with
sidekick monkey & accordion
waving a chainsaw in the air &
decide out of a certain amount
of doubt & fear to just turn
it around & head towards
higher ground & the border
where a sign reads "tijuana" as
heard the tea & weed far better
so says that sage j kerouac who
made it with all those fine kind
sweet to die for mexican angels

Aftermath/Denouement:

they are setting up the gardens & advertisements
for the sacrifice & slaughter, the young clean-cut
cookiecutter soldiers with all their pride & gusto,
the idiot tourists & young lovers—a closeup
of beauty queens & baton twirlers & bombs
being paraded down the center of town with
flowers & military flyovers to proudly show
off all their raw might & power, ready-made
reporters with their plastic expressions
the diplomats & dictators like some
incestuous human pyramid of who-

you-know nepotism, glossy pie charts
& signs set up *by design* which indicate
new high rise condominiums with well-
equipped doormen who represent lost
father figures & what it means to feel
safe & secure & live in the lap of luxury
as well as that happily-ever-after might
over right principle of kill or be killed
self-determination & autonomy; pristine,
climate-controlled, air-conditioned, muzac-
playing mall & promenade, specially retro-
fitted for functioning, forward-thinking
citizen with kitsch cafes & restaurants &
souvenir shop postcard carousels, exclusive
posh shoe shops & jewelry stores & a very
neat & tidy & thin & tall pusillanimous
philanthropic man with a pasted-on grin (bin
of prepackaged bureaucrats & board members)
& gigantic set of scissors getting ready for token
ribbon-cutting ceremonies to usher in a whole
new holy age of health clubs & mental health
clinics—everything you could possibly ask for
& more or less & who would ever guess there's
about to be over the airwaves which includes
the tv & radio all for your own personal
listening pleasure & enjoyment
& entertainment a bloody massacre
& sacrifice & slaughter in one of the most
cultured civilized wealthiest countries per-capita

Profile:

is it just me but do not all these people
running for a position in trump's cabinet
look like those psychotic stuffed puppets

come to life in the middle of the night in your
grandma's plastic wrapped house in oceanside?

the commander-in-chief in his uproarious press conference
simply points at a little girl in her pretty polka-dotted dress
with her sweet, meek voice innocently asking "why are you
doing these things? we need you, don't worry still love you"

Before:

suddenly realized
        as it hit me
                that trump
     is that gameshow host
from that 1970's gameshow
              "let's make a deal"
            while the screaming
                      seething audience
          are all the brain
               washed fools
                      who voted for him
  & you're given
            the ridiculous ultimatum
                   of that shiny object
     or what's behind the curtain
& like that 'odd couple' episode
             end up with a life
                    time supply of squid

After:

rather his recent selection of cabinet
members with the television barker
uncontrollably hollering out loud
"come on down!" and they come
psychotically barreling down the

aisle, arms flailing, eyes bulging out
the sockets (in ten-gallon and sequins)
the idiot tv audience going mad "so tell
us a little bit about yourself?"—i used to
traffic minors and have sex with teenage
girls—i want to remove fluoride from
the water supply and get rid of the polio
vaccine—i used to cozy-up with such
famous strongmen putin and assad and
got to really know them on a personal
level until you realize they're all just
a bunch of brainwashed madmen who
want to proverbially blow it all up and
trade it all in for what's behind the infamous curtain
you wonder when will amerika be led by a bodhisattva?

Dx:

one wonders if trump has that psychological disorder
of tourette's where can't control the shit that leaves
his mouth or just a spoiled little rotten brat who's
always been 'bailed' out and never had to face any
sorta consequences insulting and offending everyone
around him while referring to mexicans as criminals
and gang members and rapists neighbors to the north
wanting to annex them and make them a 51st state
being the real estate mogul that he is converting all
of gaza to the 'middle eastern riviera' referring to
senator elizabeth warren who proudly says she's
part native-american as pocahontas our veterans
as suckers and losers wants to literally bomb all
the foreign oil fields and turn them into *exxon
mobil* practically alienating all of our allies and
cozying up with dictators couldn't make this shit
up but the whole absurd irony to this all how
he made his killing in the "hospitality" field

Addendum:

one wonders if in the land of the free
home of the brave the night before
dialogue sounded something along
the lines of 'honey have you ironed
my federal agent jumpsuit?
where's my fbi windbreaker?
my camouflage and gun?'
like curly stooge asking
has anyone seen my
squirting carnation
on the morning of
older distinguished
republican (trying to
look like richard burton)
gets his face spray painted
orange to look younger for
the tv cameras and public
and podium; you preferred
so much more those shots
of albert anastasia sprayed
with bullets in that barber shop
chair as just seemed so much
more convincing and sincere

the price of eggs still soaring
and *waffle house* having to add
a 50 cent surcharge for customers

Klinical Con/clueless

i do hope when trump buys back
the panama canal puts up his own
personalized brand of condominiums
award-winning 18 hole golf course &
whole stripmall of drive-thru fast food

pharmacies & cathedrals where
over speakers can conveniently
make confessions while picking up
your prescription depending on your
condition of liquid methadone a jug
of *manischewitz* or pint of *mad dog*

V.

just the absurd freakin' fact
that half this country would
actually vote for this freak
show act with a whole rap
sheet which runs from bank
fraud to attempting to over
throw the government to
sexual violation to tax
evasion to 'invasion
of the body snatchers'
while a rich spoiled kid
with a psychological hx
most likely would never
ever once say he's wrong
or sorry or admit to cutting
down one those cherry trees
(worshiping & looking up
to late-great fake tailgunner
joe mccarthy lawyer roy cohn)
to try & get as many dead
presidents as he can all
built off the sweat of
other men & still never
once pay them & after
one of his wives got
pregnant did purchase
one of those porn stars

'hush' little baby
don't say a word
this amerika who
you're voting for?

VI.

the next president of the united states of amerika
should be like one of those old timers with shirt
always off on the boardwalk and transistor radio
perched on his shoulder pasted to earlobe wasted
and wired with the news of the whole warped and
wild world, like old man buddha, bald-headed black
man getting a good sweat going with a soaking towel
over his dome squatting in front of a casino in reno
the shattered cabinet composed of something of a
circus-like freakshow, that overgrown arthritic man
on splintered stilts, his sister been cheated on way too
many times before by life and the one she truly loved,
infamous morbidly-obese lady who's grown
out her beard—brother who can't stay out
of trouble, and dwarf all dressed up in his
dwarf uniform laying on his back with a
tear in his eye and drinking problem all now
holed-down in that classic ole brokendown
weatherworn sandcastle hotel overlooking
the shore all once with serious mental
health problems of sorts and thus
know what it's like to truly struggle
and suffer and sincerely feel alone
in this world while have the uncanny
ability and humanity and potential to
enact and pass universal laws and that
there will all represent our next true-blue
president of the united states of amerika
that old timer with his shirt eternally off

and transistor radio religiously stuck to ear
like some weird awkward translator trying
to make sense of it all with all that static
like the sound of the waves crashing back
& forth on shore and that whole freakshow
cabinet who at last sincerely care and give
a damn about the fate of the free world

VII.

in the morning watching one of those leftover infomercials
you find yourself intrigued by that absurd linguistic term
wondering its origins and derivation and where it came
from "foolproof" while ironically now in the so-called
greatest democracy in the world have a present day
candidate for president of the united states standing
in front of the tv hawking bibles for $60 a pop
to pay off for his criminal and court fees claiming
country needs more christianity while remember
that brilliant movie back in the 70's "paper moon"
where the slick & smooth ryan o'neil played a fast
talking grifter (with his adorable daughter) selling
bibles up & down the backroads of great depression
amerika taking advantage of recent poor widows and
think wow how things have really not changed that much
and yes how history does have a tendency to repeat itself

VIII.

do they ever have booing for
crepe eraser infomercials?
where's the crepe myrtle?
those mini olive-green
military action heroes
elvis down on knee

beautiful rain falls
in the morning . . .

IX.

people like that (infamous phonies)
just simply make you feel real lonely
like some relentless endless pitch from
some sleazy bullshit used car salesman
why you used to just take off from your flat
in the lower east side no matter the weather
rain snow the brutal beautiful fall and stroll
all the way to that $2 theater in hell's kitchen
(even if they came out 6 months later) and
watch films all day (sometimes crazy even
better during the holidays) and when you
left practically everything forgotten drifting
back through the smoking sewers steamy
laundromats as if at last nothing had ever
happened your own "brand" of forgiveness
when "dealing" with those types of people

X.

Frame 1

we have the whole wide world tragically
disappearing & melting away due to global
warming—those gorgeous giant polar bears
sailing away on chunks of broken off pieces
of ice but still amerika manages to sell you
(through the blatant act of advertising)
save your soul & rescue you & make
you feel a bit better about yourself for
the time being over your tv some brand
new bottle of instant spot remover or the best

vacuum cleaner ever with the strongest suction
real people real results—important to note
was a brilliant tragic comic episode some
time ago of the stooges where curly lugged
a gigantic piece of ice all the way up a huge
flight of stairs (probably somewhere around
black & white great depression san francisco)
& when he got to the top after all that hard
work & struggle much to his chagrin &
bewilderment all had suddenly melted left
with just that pair of rusty tongs & puddle

Frame 2

alas in the land of amerika they'll show
you just about as much in a shampoo
commercial as they can to keep you
under the influence like the secret
dropping of bombs all for the sake of oil
& to make the world safe for democracy
—some seductive mermaid-like lady
with her long mythological flowing
hair slowly rubbing it all in going
down from top to bottom only as
far as the camera is willing to take
you (ironically after vietnam they're
no longer allowed to show any images
of war) so just beware when you are
seduced by that beautiful woman in
the shower know they gave you just
as much as they 'humanly' possibly
could to purchase the product even
more than the killing & murder of
1000's of innocent women & children

Frame 3

amerika always seems so organized
& gung-ho when it comes down to
entering war yet not so much so when
gotta exit & take off, while a couple
years later (when everything's cooled
off) have these very formal broadcast
interrogations over news stations
to try & scapegoat & pin blame on
innocent victims or govern/mental
agencies to prove that it's not just that
infamous proverb of "might over right"
or 'curiosity' but also complacency which
killed the cat & more than likely ironically
that whole thing from the get that started it

Frame 4

why is everything in amerika
always right up in your face?
they should put a gun and
razorblade in your *taco bell*
box stuffed with tacos burritos
and quesadillas. i asked my rommate
how was the movie and he told me
it felt like it was made to try and
make the audience flinch and
totally got what he was saying

Frame 5

way back when when you had like that 'big brother'
motion picture association who judged and determined
(and censored) what would do damage to the human
psyche and collective-unconscious divvying out their

mandated ratings with pithy acronyms like the forbidden
"r" where you might catch a little flesh or have a curse
word slip out here and there "pg" for parental guidance
always found that linguistically fascinating like what
exactly did that entail like did you have to go home
for parental guidance and once you got it did they
then let you in or did you have to bring the actual
parent to prove it but what if that aforementioned
parent never had it themselves a "g" rating for like
those happy-go-lucky disney movies like "benji"
or "super dad" or pure harmless escapism like
having dick van dyke gleefully dancing through
the parks of london in "mary poppins" to lift spirits
to keep all of culture and civilization brainwashed
and placated and contented or that newly added
one of an "nc17" where absolutely no one no body
in any body spirit shape or form below the age of 17
may be let in as may expose them to a little frontal
nudity and all the damage it may very well bring
causing the youth and adolescent to start feening
and act-out and parrot that selfsame behavior and
even go out and commit some kind of taboo sex act
"x" won't even get into that originally intended for
such flicks like "midnight cowboy" and "last tango in
paris" some of my favorites which in my opinion found
to be some of the most absorbing and moving and tran-
scendent and leaving the theater feeling like a new man

Frame 6

porn stars with handlebar moustaches
play golf in the swaying shadows
of the palms not very much different
than one of those successful ceo's always
with the right thing to say saying nothing
at all difficult making any sorta distinction

(both out for self) who contributes more to
the community wondering how they're going
to pay off wife & mortgage and keep everyone
happy—at the drugstore souvenir shop picking
up that suntan lotion with paba glossy magazines
and postcards and a paperback from the tourist
carousel to take off to a whole other world

Frame 7

i wanna take a trip
with my wife to vegas
does *the tropicana* still exist?
then the local express to bali
like those honeymoon pics
on lake lugano when cute
as a button her beach
hat kept blowing off

Frame 8

let me just die a happy man
with dunkin munchkin in hand
& coconut crumbs in my beard
bottle ancient palm wine beneath the sphinx
crawling out the sea one of the first solitary
creatures & amphibians from that infamous
stage of evolution onto the pristine beaches
of antigua to the leftover tin drums
from the drunken night before
them saying how much i resemble lenin
first name always forgotten hung up by
a couple clothespins overlooking all of
beautiful bleary-eyed sunrise brooklyn
going to those bible club
meetings buzzed off malt liquor

a grandfather clock going through
a mid-life crisis counting down
the daze minutes moments
reflecting on past girlfriends
for all the right & wrong reasons
how trekking through ancient ruins
no different than those transcendent
configurations of curious childhood
instead of a stone left on tombstone
a bacbka & a dozen salt bagels for the
puerto rican gravediggers & my irish-italian
boss who gave me my first break at bookstore
a book of stretches for the upcoming apocalypse
& how to build a dinosaur out of chicken bones
in my mausoleum i'm gonna have some
humble soft spoken mexican gardener
hardworking taking care of his family
a jukebox which plays good ole ragtime
by lowdown down & out artists you never
heard before with a slavic super just there
to fix it when it breaks down with a drinking
problem but passed-down passed-out tradition
which helps him to get by in this cruel existence
the same blind man with metal detector
nodding-out at sunset & a very tall thin
redhead in tight blue jeans with high top
sneakers who makes all the brutal bullshit
& ridiculous repetition of this life & our
time on earth just a little bit more bearable
these days my life has boiled down to a manic
rapport between dummy & ventriloquist with
all parts & roles being interchangeable & not
a single soul following through on their word
having to rely on first instinct & sixth
sense to get me through all this mess
cowards do their shit from a distance
in unity there's imitation & repetition

the hitmen who just were not good shots
suffering from munchausen & melancholia
hustlers hanging out in one of those ole time
chinese restaurants with the beaded curtains
overlooking the whole misty willamette river
with stray timber floating to the great unknown
that warm washcloth tossed over sulking skull
after some great pu-pu platter szechuan feast
& only take off after figure out the heart
& soul & solve the problems of the world
that lucky number never quite rubbed off
beneath the ash resin of some lottery
ticket & left anonymous & contented
with all those black women playing
bingo in the poverty-stricken
dusk churches of coney island
the only one who feels reliable
the portly chimney sweep who
cleans our wood burning stove
& keeps his word & actually
shows up to appointments
making good casual conversation
& whenever bends over revealing
his butt crack making my wife
& i crack up in the background
the ex-con who seems so much
more honest & ironically can
trust so much more than those
crunchy know-it-all con men
always with their built-in excuses
& things they can do & not do at
their own & your inconvenience
the wallpaperer fulfilling all the
wishes dreams & fantasies of
lost lonesome suburban women
with the changing seasons & all
of american hx blowing past windows

batmobile prowls the evening parking
its long sleek fins at the drive-in to the
wail of wild wolves in the distance &
a very old stoic slavic woman who
never grins in her booth & collects
tickets as will soon all go pornographic
while through the twilight forest is some
lost sputtering town full of lumberjacks
& fugitives from the reservation with
warrants out on them & some chinese
buffet where they all congregate & those
intimate insane relationships which ended
bad mending & healing wounds over mai
tais in front of giant goldfish & boneless
seraphim to find survival of the fittest
is all just about maintaining & self
preservation & not falling under
the influence of those people &
things that cause us to feed into
self-fulfilling prophecies eventually
falling asleep to that stimulating feast
& a buzz & memories of that girl you
once were head over heels in love with
the projectionist huddled like plato's
parable in darkened cave flickering
funnel of light projecting images
& celluloid stars onto movie
screen in hopes to heal & cure
(even forgive & forget a little)
ailing population's real-life
collective-unconscious
subconscious nightmare
freudian doubts & fears
in a constant state of flux
action-adventure swashbuckler
sex symbol slapstick comedians
that freak movie usher wandering

home taking shortcuts through
ole time sacred cobblestone alleys
past a wax museum & funeral home
making absolutely no distinction at all
some laughing imbecile finally getting
eternal punchline several years later
the absent-minded carrier pigeon
delivering the wrong messages
love letters never sent to girlfriends
cuz not sure which one would take
me serious like that operator i met
& swear kept on calling me back
& proposing to hook up in atlantic city
halfway between brooklyn & philadelphia
those bulletproof bracelets & truth lasso
sold on *ebay* by wonder woman from the
penthouse of her welfare hotel which only
goes to show in the long-run everything must go
discovered in prince's elevator lo & behold
finally at last getting a good night's rest
somewhere between a butterfly
& caterpillar to the soothing
sounds of bossa-nova
a stalker never quite
having the guts
discovered with
a fluff & peanut butter
sandwich flashlight copy
of mad magazine & dsm-iv
that disorder where you feel
sympathy for your hostage
taker but got enough street
smarts & wisdom where you
see through all his disguises
& beat him at his own game
& eventually in the long-run
get one over on him while

in the very end find yourself
chasing both the garbage man
& ice cream man off the dead
end somewhere between
fact & fantasy virtue & sin
young opera singer
who used to belt
choruses beneath
the floor of your
futon & turn you
on & was the rich
jewish daughter
of some eccentric
father in philadelphia
who invented those
partitions in coffins
to keep out the
underworld
& separate
heaven
from hell
& used to
seductively
hang her wet
panties & brazzers
on clothesline outside
your sundown window
in the fading church bells
& foghorns of brooklyn
the half-crazed coroner
making silly googly eyes
like the bumbling not so
wise inspector clouseau
cuckoo clocks on strike
cuz the union told them
so & now just bow their
domes like poor rebbes

at the wailing wall
like buddha
like old broken men
just sitting in barrooms
in portland oregon cuz
got nowhere else to go
girl at the dairy cream
in a form of puppy love
saying i was a good man
you just don't know him
so let me just die a happy
man like some petrified
fish skeleton suddenly
discovered in the sand
when seagulls make
their final stand
shrug their shoulders
& just take off with
wild cacophonous
caws & alas got
no worries anymore
naturally vanishing
with the hypnotic
rhythm & rhyme
of the ocean somewhere
between fact & folklore

Frame 9

you get lowered under with those old faded scars
you used to be so self-conscious of when as an
overzealous boy literally flew straight through
locked glass kitchen door hollering "superman!"
falling onto the porch—your mandated therapist
asking you your first lucid memories on the planet
earth and telling him this, as well as constantly

seeing richard millhouse nixon's thick five o'clock
shadow plastered all over the *zenith* television with the
caption of "watergate" having no idea what it was all about

Real-Life Denouement

when they lower you under the faceless telemarketer
reading directly off the telemarketer script will very
politely say in her placating trained voice press 1
if you've put a bullet in you brain press 2 if we've
caused you to go slowly insane press 3 if your
loved one does not validate and just made you
feel even lonelier with absolutely no one to turn
to press 4 if can't get to door and are a harm
to yourself or others press 5 if no longer alive
press 6 if do not exist press 7 if believe in hell
or heaven press 8 if feel existentially raped
press 9 due to all the bullshit and lies and
false advertising enough to drive any good
man mad press 10 to allow us to get to know
you better what are your dreams and nightmares
what are your hobbies and who are your superheroes
and villains who should we contact in case of emergency
do you mind if visiting angel smokes and smells of tobacco?

Frame 10

u wonder if you're just starting
        to become like one
                of your old pals
  u grew up with
        (now on facebook)
                somewhere
                      between
                            suicidal & homicidal

just trying to get by
    on a daily basis
        like when u
            finally found out
                how he used to
try & run over
    squirrels due to
        some sorta
            desertion
                abandonment
& his father never
    being around
        would help to explain
            why when went
                over to house
        one morning
            saw that poor bird
                we were trying
                    to nurse back
                        to health
  in a converse sneaker box
      swinging from the rafters
            why he tells me
                now how he will
                    never watch
                        college football
            probably
              due to
              similar reasons
& will go on cruises
    like every other
        , suburbanite
            in amerika
                with his wife
                    & daughters
            & in a smartphone pic
  show off psychotic

    plastic smile
               after returning back
                    from his excursion
                        right outside the ship
       with a beer
brown bagging it

Frame 11

consider a case study
of a rich kid who used to live
in the old marx brother's mansion
and seemed to have something
of a death wish taking flying
leaps from way atop the staircase
dad was something like the secretary
to the shah and used to get escorted
around by his butler who spoke spanish
and hilariously cursed at him under his
breath when he used to throw temper tantrums
when he used to throw his racquet at the tennis net
and didn't give a shit and couldn't control his feelings
or emotions most likely due to an absent father figure

Frame 12

AP (history): are there any brave courageous souls
left who will stand up against mad corrupt presidents
like that protagonist in melville's brilliant short story
"bartleby the scrivener" who declares over and over again
(through passive-resistance) "i prefer not to." those authors
back then were so damn deep, keen, satirical and transcendent

Frame 13

amerika what next? what next?
some drive-by assassin going
at breakneck speed with baseball
cards clattering in the spokes of
his bicycle hunched over (superhero
style) on his banana seat with flower
basket ringing his mini bell like mad
backpack with bloody bow & arrow
protein bars and manifestoes racing
like the wind for his last supper at
the golden arches and all those women
online willing to save and support him
lost bridesmaids who will marry him
and give him a couple kids in prison
all turned into a best seller and mini
series streaming on *disney* & *hulu*?

XI.

so god bless amerika what else can we do
but celebrate another holiday mourn another
mass-killing or set off an m-80 in a dumpster
to trigger your post-traumatic stress disorder
or some routine & ritual righteous reenactment
of some battle where some very earnest sentimental
minuteman dressed to kill shoots off his long rifle
with a whole mess of morbidly-obese tourists in
souvenir sunglasses just standing in the back
ground having no idea what it's all about so
why not just put hand on your brain/washed
man/dated heart to try & prove & show off
what a feeling reality show soul you really
are while caught looking down at your smart
phone in the middle of the mass throng cookie
cutter crowd & when they do a closeup show

what a really scary wannabe violent bully
automaton you are with your pre/meditated
pre/manufactured quasi threatening body
language & moves twitching & jerking
out-of-control uh-o straight from the 'burbs
man, used to have so much more respect for
them when did the bunnyhop & cha-cha-cha

XII.

the referee stands all alone
in the middle of the logo
for *the cheez-it bowl*
while some offensive
caricature of an
american indian
with his shirt off
and warpaint on
rides wildly bareback
across the field flamboyantly waving
spear right there in mid-air inspiring
a whole soulless student body to start
making mock chops with tomahawks
and some dumb ass white girl from the
sorority without a care in the world to take
a picture of herself over her smartphone.
you lean back in your easy chair strangely
enough thinking of margerie schnur
ultra-orthodox jewish girl who used
to flirt with you undercover taboo
working fully to her advantage
during statistics at yeshiva
while now just feel this
overwhelming sensation
of solitary confinement
of feeling so alone like

waiting in some waiting
room for your lie detector
test or a mini-mental for
possible dementia both
pretty much a moot point
as feel numb all over, while
the tv screen ironically reads
"bowl mania." you do your
own personal reflection back
on the year in amerika and
what first comes to mind
or gets triggered is how
this entertainment park
got busted over tourists'
cell phones where the friendly
happy-go-lucky animal mascot
refused to hug any of the black
kids running towards him, and
only when they finally got faced
with natural consequences, the
only way the black man can
finally prove he exists, puts
out some phony patronizing
public apology how this runs
purely antithetical and contrary
to their 'all-inclusive ethical policy'
and now will supply those african-
american families with their token
coupons and free admission
over any weekend to show
their contrition and how
they're so family-oriented
(not of course factoring in any
natural long-term psychological
hardwired trauma and damage).
you head back in after half
time to the cheez-it bowl

where surprisingly oklahoma
holds a commanding lead over
florida state "fighting seminoles"

XIII.

art rimbaud turns
low lowdown lost
down in the dumps
like that once thoughtful
tearful american indian
reflecting about the state
of the present day floridian
with their stand-me-ground
pocket knife pistol & opiate
problem chemically dependent
mickey mouse suicidal cinderella
working per-diem waiting on line
bumpadabumpa at the drive-thru
pharmacy for their prescription
at the drive-thru chapel making
their drive-thru confessions hoping
to be absolved of their sins heading
back in their climate-controlled air-
conditioned vehicles to their condominium
complex (past those majestic immaculate
supermarkets its inhabitants take great
pride in making actual stock investments)
not like he once imagined it to be in the
primitive pristine holy sacred *floridas*
while when he gets back will get a surf
& turf platter delivered (by a very young
intense impressionable lud wittgenstein)
immune to the news on that mini tv
keeping him company in the kitchen
during those erratic swings of emotion

reporting about just another down
to earth all-american hero being
brought up on corruption charges
as doesn't seem all that far from
when he took off & ranaway from
his bore/joi suburb for a life of
action & adventure as a wild genius
child while through the barren blinds
of his unit spying rich daughters
(all loose & liberal) doing bong
hits around the community pool

XIV.

they said that the infamous author henry miller
at the end of his life suffered from severe bouts
of nightmares as if even after getting through
all that suffering and struggle and becoming

something of a success his past literally
came back to haunt him while appears
like the human mind deep down inside
just will never let up and never ever

quite get over all that loneliness as in
this case could never really proverbially
escape new york like those little slight
cracks still in the sidewalk and weeds
managing to push their way through

an interesting phenomenon when my wife
first got pregnant with our child was how
i started dreaming all over again and hadn't
done so for ages just busy trying to survive
and get by in life and when i all of a sudden
started having these very clear and lucid
dreams of my bittersweet childhood

so maybe it might just be recommended
to take after that old timer who still goes
into work each and every day in that blue
blazer still going through the motions standing
with his age-old briefcase on the edge of the
platform now only working a couple hours
a day at that stock firm or advertising agency

all the clean-cut young bucks kidding around
with him making fun of what's in that briefcase
and him loving it with those silent humble
expressions washing over his face feeling
that sense of belonging and being a part
of things and that supposed team or family

heading back home early to *grand central*
still clean and empty before all the craziness
of rush hour as well as the silent surreal local
when he takes that zooming train back
to the suburbs; may even have some

time to help out his lovely wife in the
garden who always stood by his side
still experiencing the keen palpable
sensation of the change of seasons
and trains rattling and whooshing
like the wind in the distance. . .

those lovely maples maintenance keeps
in such good shape with those gigantic
regenerating leaves you can rely on
to come out year after year to provide
those sheltering shadows which might escort him
back to where he originally came from and all started

If p

last minute on the spur
of the moment took off
with that borderline girl
smart & wild as hell
from her flat in sleepy
hollow during christmas
break at *wurzweiler school
of social work* & in one
fell swoop took the road
as far south as it'd take
us made it down the pike
to the city of brotherly
love the brooding lincoln
memorial where you had
a secret sacred rapport
over the mason-dixon
& swear felt all those
ancient spirits from
young civil war soldiers
to where wilbur & orville
took off from around kill
devil hills outer banks of
the carolinas had never
been to before in the
off-season & just standing
on the terrace in the brilliant
morning hearing her blissfully
hollering about that infamous dolphin
spotted until you just realized this life
& reality simply made up of moments
you must never ever take for granted

Then q

truck driving memories of being
all alone 20 years old in the midnight
hills of portland, oregon and this older
woman truck driver (still very attractive)
just giving me her extra coat (with this
wonderful natural nurturing quality)
thought i was cold and felt like some
thing like seeing me as being her long-
lost son and in many ways i was and
thankful and grateful and it's memories
& moments like this that still last forever

XV.

how dreams can tear you apart like visions
of that ex-con doing pull-ups on that streetlight
on the corner after coming out of prison—i've done
practically every job under the sun while remember
interviewing for one from this dentist i swear ain't
making this up something like picking up and
delivering patients' teeth through the mountains
of the berkshires telling me he refused to hire me
cuz saw a scar on my arm convinced i was some
sort of dope addict when in fact i had at that point
in my life worked three jobs at a time just to pay
my room and board out in portland oregon putting
up cubicles for this pharmaceutical company donating
my blood with my downtime and learning to drive a truck
at dusk as the guy was such an arrogant know-it-all schmuck
and even told him if he wanted to look up my records at this
blood bank turning me into an instant hardened criminal when
willing to go all out for him—talk about knowing the ins & outs
of culture on every level while funny grew up the son of a dentist

XVI.

you think back then when you used to go on
those escape missions from the homeowners
association & would drive miles to the ocean
& quite often see like these giant turtles sincerely
& in great earnest struggling to cross the sandy
road & would enthusiastically jump out my car
& gingerly pick them up & place them in that part
of the swampy high grass making sure they were
alright while tell you in that moment nothing felt
better as for good & necessary reason had
blocked out all those killers back in suburbia
with manic episodes of cheating & betrayal on
neighbors & best friends & wives & husbands
& all those cases of rabid alcoholism from
judges to spoiled sons who owned their
daddy's auto body shop & threatening
to kill each other & each others dogs
literally ironically barking aloud
doing their daily call to the cops
being these little life insurance agents
with napoleonic complexes while all you
cared about in the moment was just helping
out that poor tortoise trying to cross the road

XVII.

suburbia is false advertising (stop) pure illusion & hysteria (stop)
the closer you get to that body of water or ocean the more successful
(stop) the better & finer the stonework (stop) there's never anyone out
on their lawns (stop) just the landscapers to make sure it's all manicured
& meticulous & perfect (stop) signs of life every so often seeing some
stray jogger with that lost desperate nondescript look on their face (stop)
as if pacing themselves to meet their maker (stop) that country club which
will insure your entrance into the pearly gates (stop) accept or reject you
based on whether the right class race or religion (stop) but i was sure i was

virtuous (stop) i think i am i think i am i think i am (stop) freedom dragging
those garbage cans all the way to the end of your driveway (stop) & better
make sure you put them in the exact right spot (stop) while ironically pulling
out your junkmail & returning back to the starting point & flipping through it
to prove how indifferent (stop) how exclusive (stop) turning on your television
at the bewitching hour to get all of tomorrow's rush hour weather (stop) if suffer
from insomnia got family court which will instantly judge & determine whether
you get into hell or heaven (stop) with that whole pathetic pack of a studio
audience mass mob mentality jury (stop) & hope & pray it may all end up
being like some free glossy tom selleck glossy catalog with one of those
reverse mortgages which will measure your means & mortality (stop)
suburbia all false advertising (stop) pure illusion & hysteria (stop)

XVIII.

considering the recent bleak nature of my
life these days and people just being such
a bunch of goddamn flakes would happily
welcome kato showing up in his ninja
outfit for his surprise visit going in for
the kill—at least he's trustworthy and
reliable and sincere in his conviction
nowadays the messenger wouldn't
even make it making their feeble
built-in excuses and wouldn't even
find out the status of rosencrantz
& guildenstern rhoda morgenstern

XIX.

after they deported chaplin
back to the shores of england
how long did it take till he was
allowed to come back and visit
pick up a dozen bagels
lox & whitefish a nice

pastrami sandwich &
dr. brown's cream soda
at katz's delicatessen
on delancey not
terribly far from
where that old
lady mannequin
played piano in the
window of that music
store on orchard
the rest of his
ashcan ozzy
look-alike
ancestors
in hobo
clothes
beneath the
brooklyn bridge
for different but
very similar reasons
your mom who grew
up on pitt street &
grandfather who
worked in the
garment district
every other sunday
surprising her
by giving her a bag
of panties & bag of candy
for some strange reason
go figure hx of amerika

XX.

courage kept calling u
& never once ever did u
shy away from it even if
it meant climbing up the
steps of a *greyhound* as
a young kid & taking off
from *port authority station*
all by your lonesome out
to frisco reno portland
living in such fleabag
motels like the *jack london*
with drag queens & killers
finding yourself nodding-
out from exhaustion at some
woolworth counter in montana
in the imagination of the pharmacy
counter of your grandfather's from
bedford stuyvesant brooklyn who
literally sold heroin & ice cream
sodas just to make this whole
goddamn lonesome fucked-up
messed-up life a little bit better

XXI.

AP: a miracle happened. peace finally broke out
in the madhouse of congress and the politicians
were actually found doing their jobs while not
only did they cross the aisle but husbands and
wives from opposing parties were found waltzing
with each other. guns and grudges checked in with
the hat check girl. rival senators were purchasing
shots for each other. children were playing classic
old-fashioned games on the south lawn like pin the
tail on the donkey, snap the whip, and enthusiastically

hollering–"red rover, red rover, let ___ come over!"
and similar to how almost all great dramas end that
classic which always used to get played over and
over again by the dj at disco bar-mitzvahs donna
summer's "last dance, last dance for love . . ."

XXII.

outside you sit back in your office swivel chair
looking down on the whole damn blessed long
gone lewis & clark alcatraz pacific ocean your
free guidebook on how to improve your *wrigley's*
smile without even trying keats shelley kerouac
cantos your giant leftover burrito & *mad dog
cool breeze 20/20* while gotta roundup all the
cantaloupe farmers & get them back over the
border as soon as possible as equate to all those
rapists & gang members (those single women
with cats & haitians feasting on man's best friend)
man how the great amerikan dream has become so jaded
& deranged & turned to such evil dynamics of brainwash
& hallucination not making enough space for those smiling
caucasians cemented beneath highrise concrete condominiums

08

god—if warhol spoke of that 15 minutes of fame
what do you make of these present-day politicians
like the remains of some insane classless class reunion

09

i always pondered those never once taught
to say "sorry" or "thank you" then thought a little

more about it & turned off & got instantly disinterested
in those who made it a habit & living to try & hurt others

10

i find the grand metaphor for life
those faceless producers just sitting
back in the theater while those poor
starving artist-actors are giving it their
best shot desperately trying to convince
them they're the right ones for the part
from all that real-life drama from all that
loss from an experienced damaged past
and them very casually, nonchalantly
saying without a sincere bone in their
body "we'll get back to you" you
wonder if in fact there is a heaven
and hell they're eventually forced
to judge themselves just waiting on
some long line never quite getting in

11

~

object-permanence as a kid "the mod squad"
every friday at 8:00 with that whole trio of
young good looking undercover detectives
running away in that dark underground
shadowy tunnel through the puddles
running away and trying to escape
like some nightmare from something
never quite sure of nihilistic eternal
which always made you just a little
more scared as how could anyone

possibly be running away from
themselves then they'd suddenly
be in freeze-frame (right before the
commercial) making it all that much
more mysterious and existential giving
you the time to brood and wonder and
think about it a little longer while they
were always so earnest and sincere
and serious and down-to-earth as
this must be what was the essence
of the human soul always wondering
if they ever found that thing they
were running away from and
looking for—themselves

~

good dreams can be had too
forgetting the dream just leaving
you with that really good feeling
which is the transcendent soul
standing proudly by mom
in a polaroid at 3 years old
with a great big casual smile
in dungaree overalls (cuz this
is all life was) 1971 toddler
& 20 year old posing in
matching dungaree overalls
below those mythological *jack
in the beanstalk* stalks of corn
having grown out of control
on the side of mint-green home
ann margaret boogying with
elvis in "viva las vegas" this
season getting visited by that
lone wild turkey in your orchard
soaring past your bathroom window

& disappearing to that wild apple tree
blossoming over the fence next door

good dreams can be had as well
which is the transcendent soul . . .

∼

sunday morning in the dew
before any of the neighbors
woke up on the dead end
after infamous sleepovers
with best friend secretly
peddling your bicycles
through sleepy suburb
until arrived to a patch
of woods and walking
them through sideyards
while you made it to
carpenter's pond and
sat all day on top of the
waterfall and discussed
all your dreams for the future
whether they came true or not
completely irrelevant while
that moment lasted forever

∼

falling inn
the dewy
leaf pile
on each
& every
corner
put up
by the

gardeners
could anything
have been much better?

~

great adventures of childhood
existed in unfinished basements
backyards becoming wild forests
crossing streams which divided
civilization & the imagination

~

remember back in summer camp
how you used to have like those
navy-blue army blankets in a jelly
roll at the end of your bed? well
feel like could really use that
once again to wrap myself
in to turn all nightmares
to innocent dreaming

the counselor reading to us
treasure island when all
the lights went out . . .

never quite sure how that ended

~

back then you had legitimate heroes
like steve mcqueen & clint eastwood
paul newman & robert redford
like the remains of a stoning
returning home tipsy from
the all-you-can-eat sangria

dinner theater eating cold
chef boyardee straight from
the can with best friends and
single parents always missing
in action with their secret stash
of marijuana in a sandwich bag
the midgets (as in midget wrestling)
on this new medium called cable tv

~

surviving suburbia
was like that game
you used to play
as a child how
long able to
hold breath
under water
your mother
picking you
up later at
sundown
shivering
with blood
shot eyes
outside
the y

~

having 2
take awl
that bull
shit
non
stop
never

ending
advice
'n ad
4 vice
y we
cud
ant
stay
out
of
trubble
all that
actin
out
doin
bronx
runs
smoking
all that
gone
jah
during
summer
only
feel
ing
alive
when
due
wing
wild
mad
pool
hopping
way after
midnight
getting

dropped
off on
lawns
waste
dead
finally
at last
wit
nuth
end
left
2
live
4

~

how come the famous psychologist
erik b. erickson never had a phase
in his human stages of growth
and development where you
can go back to that first girl
in high school you had your
first wet dream to? erickson
claimed if you were not able
to get through or work through
or sublimate a particular stage
always had the opportunity to
make up and go back (to it)
during any specific period
of your life as was fluid
and flexible and could
achieve and redeem that
(as opposed to freud who
seemed pretty set in stone)
i ran into mine in the upper
east side and actually appeared

kinda excited to see me (was
a beauty and the daughter of
a diplomat who used to rub up
against me in ap history) and ended
up being married to some real schmuck
of a businessman and found myself
more than disappointed while wish
i had just stuck to that wet dream

∼

the interrogators usually just a bunch
of poor impersonators you were able
to see right through and charm them
and break them down in laughter
and usually end up talking about
wives and life and politics and
them eventually asking you if
there were any possible positions
open in the field of social work . . .

∼

stealing the teacher's edition
with all the answers in it for
that second language we were
mandated to take; the teacher
exclaiming "joey, brilliant!"
during oral session all those
kiss-ass goody-goodies
gathered around me
thinking jean-paul
at his birthday party
in those glossy photos
back in paris living
such a simpler life
while this dichotomy
what culture's truly about

~

when yer dealing
    with all that
        true-blue
            nonstop
                family dysfunction
you sincerely
    get stuck
        in one of
            those home movies
getting spun around
    wildly
        with a blindfold on
            staggering
                disoriented
  trying to pin a tail
      on that donkey
          swinging madly
              blindly
                    at that pinata
                        not sure why
          you keep on
              fulfilling
                  that self-fulfilling
                      prophecy
  bruises
      black eyes
          skinned knees
              one of those wide
                  ear to ear
                      polaroid smiles
spending your school daze
        in detention
            brooding
                reflecting
  outside warm
        spring window

                        a whole other sorta
                            mad insane
                                cock-a-mamie
                                    manifest destiny

                ~

looking back at growing up always
seemed to instantly judge me like one
of those 'wild child at-risk troublemakers'
but when they actually gave me the chance
and opportunity to get to really know me
found me to be a rather sensitive thoughtful
and down-to-earth dude who'd do practically
anything for anyone (a delinquent who was
always able to charm the moms) and remember
feeling even slightly a bit patronized by sorry
those know-it-all all-knowing phonies like tell
me something i don't know or one of those
big ole dogs who didn't have a mean bone

            ~

just bury my ole bones in that
blue *izod lacoste* alligator shirt
fresh new pair of leather *pumas*
with that great big stupid smile
& mop of mussy hair from
that polaroid down in
the magical kingdom
jesus was nailed
to the cross
not just by
coincidence
more so
the jealousy
& pettiness
& patterns

of human nature
right around christmas
jimmy stewart desperately
hollering & praying
for some sense
of fairness
& forgiveness
in the black
& white static of
"it's a wonderful life"
your first beautiful
blonde love from
the rhineland
waking up
in her arms
in a winter
wonderland
gotta work so
damn hard just
for little happiness
all stored perfectly
in the back of those
russet corduroys with
a hole in your pocket

12

all answers found & discovered on those treasure maps
of paper placemats at *the international house of pancakes*

rainy laundromats just felt like "the land of the lost" where you
got lost in a good paperback & found your long-lost soulmate

13

falling in love—

provides a whole new perspective
& natural meaning & purpose
& substance to this existence

you think of purchasing ballet tickets . . .
she tells you she hasn't been to a game in ages
with hotdogs & beer even if she doesn't mean it

the seasons (the falling leaves & snowfall)
become that much more detail-oriented as you
stroll with her to the bus stop & diner on the corner

14

the difference between the german & russian blonde
not too much when taking into account the amount of
obsessive contemplation (on an intellectual & intimate
level, what love is?) wandering the snowy suburbs
like some relentless endless forest for hours on end
during christmas vacation from college meeting up
later on at that smoky tavern on the outskirts of town

15

the essence of what true silence is
anonymous alone in the constant
still 'silent' snowfall & all those
trees & shrubs & homes taking on
the simplest of geometric shapes & forms

all that 'quiet & calm' which feels
like folklore after the madness of it all
the wingspan of snow angels at nightfall

16

those surreal images from sentimental memories
not necessarily as succinct (or clear & lucid) as
you may very well think when considering that
anguished alienating solitary & isolating phase
& period of persistent reflecting & ruminating

17

we have a tendency to romanticize all those things
contrary to what we so desperately try to escape

you steal feel like a fugitive on-the-run
being accused of a crime you know not of

18

An Abstract:

all those great existentialists railed about
life & death & existence—how do we
live & persist in a miserable world without
some great grand spirit & find happiness?
what we do with all of our freedom? all that
guilt & conflict without turning self-destructive?
that friend you grew up with found on the surface
of his pool—the name of that rolling stone too?

Before:

dealing with figures of authority
lying always seemed like the best
and most viable option & opportunity
as a child cuz by their standards (or the way
i felt about myself) was a bad boy, couldn't keep
myself out of trouble and wild, while why not keep
them rolling in the aisle (trying to win their approval
and rebelling against the rules at the exact same time
doing the rope-a-dope, fighting myself out the corner)
charming them and would never ever let them get close
or the better of me, taking advantage even if they wanted
usually in the end for the most part winning by no-decision

After:

best we can do is to prepare our children
for a life & existence phony & full of it
also too those 'starving artists' for sale
on sunday at the *airport marriott*
all those air-conditioned malls
& *bed bath & beyond* when
at last anonymous aimless
& got nowhere else to go
& need to cool off some
bumpadabumpa rush hour traffic
to the ancient ruins & acropolis
how bernard baruch made his
first million selling short on futures
who dun' it & the funnies section

Proclamation:

the key to advertising is getting
to one's core needs & fantasies
providing instant-gratification
for all those things which seem
so troubling or just out of reach
rescuing us from all that
uncontrollable obsessive
worrying & wondering
with a quasi safety
security to one's
own mortality

Proof:

Test 1.

that bossa nova muzac which interestingly
conveniently got played like half-crazed
hosannahs of angels in all those very
safe & secure home away from home
supermarkets across amerika during
the 50's to influence & seduce & soothe
the madonna-whore housewife's libido
almost putting her under some sorta
hypnotic spell to continue to purchase
food such as those tv dinners & *tang* for her
brainwashed happily-ever-after 'nuclear' family

Test 2.

back in the 50's early 60's
one of those cartoon owls
or superheroes in leotards
would just show up out

of nowhere to your
kitchen window
on television
to provide instant
panaceas & heal
all the problems
then with great
vigor & gusto
proclaim
[the healing
properties of]
the product
for both the
mother & child

Test 3.

in the 70's it was mr. whipple
planted in the aisle with that
strange psychotic pedophilic
laughter exclaiming "don't squeeze
the charmin!" freaking you out—why
probably turned to a life of kleptomania

Test 4.

in the here & now present
for sudden bouts of insomnia
in the wee hours of the night
infomercials of that madman
phil swift like that late-great
sci-fi writer or satirist healing
all your possible issues and
conflicts by simply applying
just a little bit of his miracle
adhesive to any man-made

disaster such as a leaky gutter
or one of those weatherworn
makeshift speedboats now
speeding through the bayou
literally yelling "wa-hoooo!"

Test 5.

on calling *kay jewelers* they leave you
on hold forever where keep on repeating
the same old freakin message over and
over again about topaz and all its secret
powers; how it represents courage and
integrity and honor and the renaissance
and how in india they used to wear it
over their heart and by this point just
want to blow your brains out and wonder
if back in the day when we used to watch
those early morning sunday tv shows like the
mighty *isis* or *shazam* had one for suicidal ideations

Test 6.

no one ever
    really prepares u
        for how crazy
            marriage can get
                & how it can drain u
  feel like mo—zes!
      all grownup
        being pushed
          back down
            the nile

      for rehab
          & anger management
              snickering beneath
                  the pyramids & palm trees
not sure if it's vegas
      or the sphinx
            "i'd like to buy the world a coke . . ."

Life of a Social Worker

❊ ❊ ❊

on the rebound in teacher's lounge

❊ ❊ ❊

wild boys and girls decked-out in
goggles getting it all out in woodshop

❊ ❊ ❊

that sainted boy with big blue eyes and dad in jail
doing his daily ritual of running away down the hall

❊ ❊ ❊

that charming girl whose eyes glow like pearls
& knows more than all of them put together forced
to do her daily visit at the vehement vice principals

❊ ❊ ❊

secretaries don't say a thing at all
acting as if it's for her own good

❀ ❀ ❀

a full still life of every last kid
crashing through the front doors
when that final period bell rings
while truly what freedom means

A Concrete . . .

we got brought up on pledging allegiance
and now it's the ten commandments and
got a front runner candidate for president
who broke half of them and the other half
trying to hawk the holy book for 60 dollars
a pop to pay back his court fees and all
those ladies violated and took advantage
of on the "hush hush"—amerika what is
wrong with this picture while we can do
all this ideological political and critical
analysis but what it all comes down
to in the long-run is the philosophical
parables of 'might over right' and 'is
it better to be feared or to be loved?'

Abstract

it's as if this country suffers from very
dumb convenient amnesia and forgot
all about joe mccarthy roy cohn j. edgar
hoover and that infamous blacklist and
all those lives ruined and got absolutely
no problem going back to that era again
as in my opinion greatest sin and crime
against man is ignorance and those who
simply forget or choose not to remember
while the real true-blue problem in amerika

more often is just in its citizens when they
blindly vote for their great commander
in chief with their emotional psycho
logical tendencies and mentality to
always have the need to either blame
or try to be saved (by some quasi myth
ological archetypal father figure) and
when it doesn't turn out the way they
thought it would act all angry and
devastated like one of those blind
dates where they feel manipulated
and that eventually got betrayed

amerika #1

we regret that we regret that we regret that we regret—
don't really give a shit always preferred ice coffee from *cumby's*
a double-feature of "raging bull" and "coal miner's daughter"

amerika #2

fallen crabapples getting them ready and stocking up
for the great rumble—no one shows up like gulf of
tonkin and weapons of mass-destruction so decide
instead to drop bombs on a foreign aspirin factory

amerika #3

ending a whole generation by violently blowing up
disco records in chicago stadium ironically making
it more than clear that all cultures are not included

Report Card

always had a good head on my shoulders
where the hell else would it be?
on that bus to mississippi?
that sleazy salesman
during lunchbreak
in hell's kitchen
exploring the
peepholes
of the city?
spanish
chinese
fast food
beneath
the bridge
in the
evening
throwing
welcome
home parties
for puerto ricans
just returned
from prison?
the avon lady
still doing her
rounds fluttering
long eyelashes
like some mad
hummingbird
through your
venetian blinds?
the sea be the best place
to be when decide to die
along with the fish skeletons
and whale bones and black boys

doing backflips off the boardwalk
yeah give me a shot, gyro without the sauce . . .

Help Wanted

jeezus krist walked on water
which i suppose sincerely
waz a feat in itself
i spent a majority
of mine beneath
the lake & lagoon
brooding with the
blues trying to make
it through after working
a full day with alcohawlik
crews painting widows'
homes or women who
had been embezzled
by guys they thought
they loved—when
the day was done
(license taken away)
pedaling miles just to drink
a cold one in the warm shower
—as a lost child never once ever
giving up on myself never taking
a thing for granted taking buses
trains crosscountry (with a back
pack full of poets & philosophers
while thought in fact i swear was
a criminal! in truth taking notes
through zooming sooty *greyhound*
windows) just trying to make it
i suppose too has something
to do with faith & the spiritual

Child Hood Cribnotes

1. how to put together a colorful craypaper kite
2. how to build a dinosaur out of chickenbones
3. how to function after constructing a squadron
   of ships & planes inadvertently sniffing the fumes
   of model glue ending up wasted & stoned—blue
4. how to step off a bus bleary-eyed in the morning
   of san francisco after taking it clear cross-country
   picking up a room on eddy in the tenderloin district
5. surviving off breakfast burritos & orange *cool breeze
   mad dog 20/20* trying to get reception on
   pawnshop transistor to candlestick park
   & literally hearing the crack of the bat

Forecast

M.

extreme winds
ladybugs on ceiling
and that beautiful red
head you always had
a mad crush on taking
a motel room in maine
with muted westerns

T.

that older woman who
picked you up outside
a movie theater and
took you back to her
ranch in the suburbs
where she fed you

all weekend chinese
& whiskey in bathtub

W.

that other older woman
who lived right next door
on that lake in the berkshires
making love constantly forever
never getting each other's last
names with a whole mailbox
stuffed with summer junk
mail you never claimed

Th.

that smart suicidal girl
from riverdale who spoke
fluent russian and asked you
to marry her multiple times
and just told her i couldn't
while found out i was far
more traditional & romantic
than i could ever imagine

F.

a little later on a whole
line of dripping bras
from that ballerina
hanging out your
merchant marine
fire escape window
in the borough
of brooklyn

Sat.

that black girl named sunshine
who i picked up in my taxi who
lived at the *times square hotel*
telling me stories about them
dumping off dead bodies in
the alley just trying to make
it and survive chanting in front
of that shrine of buddhist candles

Sun.

my bronx girl i met second year
of internship the only one who
could keep me laughing cracking
me up up and down 6th avenue
in manhattan strolling through
the heather gardens of cloisters
looking over the whole holy body
historical hudson river and universe

The Hospitality Field

every dusk
that summer
for inspiration
i used to listen
to 'wu tang
36 chambers'
before i started
my graveyard
working at the *pioneer
hotel* on the border of
little italy & chinatown
before i had to deal

with all that drama
the manager from
the island talking
all this garbage
about ghosts
& phantoms
& how cops
would plant
grins on
past guests
after they
kicked
the bucket
as have
the ability
to remain
elastic
for
just
that
short
while
like
some
sick
sadistic
riddle
yourself
drifting off
in the lobby
to green day's
"welcome to paradise"

Life of Leisure

i wish i had had
    the discipline & willpower
        to cheat on my wife
  & turn to beer nuts
    & gin & tonic
but instead
    became one of those
        good ole loyal leftover
          skate
            keys
    weeping in my condo
        in boca
          with the other
            lost
              locals
    from the
    garment
    district

Chump Change

how dare half these presses
    charge like reading fees
        or got these prizes
  for like 30 bucks
    or so
rather go
  to that haircutting school
      on 3rd avenue
        in the east village
  where they used to
    cut my hair
      for like $10
the $2 theater
    in hell's kitchen

                one of those rub-off
                      lottery cards
                              at *cumberland farms*
    where that really nice
          young kind polite
                morbidly-obese girl
                      goes "good luck honey!"
making the losing
      all that more memorable

On the Nature of Sport

+

how about trade a whole team for another team

+

trade a whole fan base for another fan base

+

trade a girlfriend for another girlfriend

+

trade a mother-in-law for another mother-in-law

+

trade those obnoxious sports radio hosts

+

and when you're real lost and down
in the dumps your commander-in-chief
will just be someone you never see while
simply this amorphous voice you switch to
on your dial when heading bumpadabumpa
into rush hour to a job making you miserable

+

how about trading a whole skyline for another skyline

+

a whole life for another life . . .

19

indifference ironically feels worse than betrayal
while the former deeper & the latter more shallow
paradoxically more active than all of those things
which eventually in the long-run caused a turn off

20

when the electricity ran out in that game *operation*
& could no longer be shocked by the bullshit of existence
we used it as a giant coaster to rest our mixed drinks & tv dinners

21

kamikaze air-circus flyers tailspinning into lobster roll stands
& 'life of leisure' cabins on the exclusive bourgeois ocean

22

martinis at 4 over psychotropic medication
leaving wives like windup dolls wandering
aimlessly disoriented through the backyards
of neighbors in a not so seductive suburbia

23

i've always been fascinated by that socio-cultural
phenomenon of those husbands who just let their
wives pick their clothes out for them and without
even thinking simply put them on; one wonders
at the end of their lives and got brittle bones just
drape 'them' over the end of their beds and continue
on with this routine and tradition and just sit down in front
of their dressing room mirror to apply their token make
up to keep the whole happily-ever-after illusion going
stability is highly overrated while trying to meet
its expectations, criteria, style of living & state
of being; maintaining develops even a more
absurd, surreal, delusional quality; internal
organs & narcotics getting delivered through
midnight mountains to the ocean where the
clinics & carnival have the best reputation

24

hypocrites always seem to conveniently
show up to come up to you during some
ceremony like your wedding to offer you
sound advice (more like hearing the sound
of their voice) from all the fucked-up things
they've [not] done in their life; how things not
quite right between them & their wife (to forgive
themselves & justify like some kind of male rite
of passage) or due to guilt & conflict trying to get
something off their chest like a drunk at confession

25

has there ever been
a condolence card created
after a failed suicide attempt
"so sorry to hear he made it"
with that oj with *some pulp*
        & those newly-discovered
                        secret capsules
     of fish oil
        from the top-secret
               land of new zealand
during an infomercial
       at 3:46 in the morning
             save your soul
                   with absolutely no need
             at all
        to move down
     to the sunshine state
           like that made-for tv
               madman doctor
          strolling double-time
      in that
   retirement community

    getting ready
             for the early evening
                      very off off broadway
                                production of "grease"

26

the best thing
after i got married
was moving out the big city
& taking a social work job
on school st. in newport
rhode island & during
lunch break just driving
freely with no one bothering
me (to me that's what real freedom
was) down that row of *cottages* or
ole time industrialist mansions & just
sitting back in that same secret spot
overlooking the choppy atlantic
eating a sandwich listening to
sports radio from manhattan
with absolutely no desire
to return to the planet

Fig. 1

how your identity these days
(all seems controlled by some secret
centralized office out in the heartland
iowa american ally like the philippines)
will break you down bone by bone rip out
your heart & soul as these days your whole
being & reality based simply on your bank
info or social & once they got that got it all

& go in for the kill & these are the ones supposedly
protecting you & empowering you with all those
popups from the heartland & iowa & manila

Fig. 2

so apparently these days god
has become like some widget
or cog who knows it all & all
your info based on some mini
microchip manufactured by
some poor peasant living
just below the poverty-line
usually in some kind of third
world country reading you
your rights directly off
the telemarketer script

Fig. 3

once a year take your
mandated annual trek
to the mall (full of perverted
old men & nymphomaniac girls)
to purchase a whole mess more of megabytes
to restore your faith & belief in man & the world

Fig. 4

the state
of
amerika
theez
daze
seems

to b
who
puts on
the best
act in
showing
guilt
&
remorse
after
getting
caught
kicking
the shit
out of
their
girl
friend
on the
last
resort
security
cameras
"i take full
responsibility"
no in fact you
really don't
by just
repeating
this quasi
moralistic
trope
written
up by
lawyer
to placate
the public

not awe/flee
con/vin/sing

Fig. 5

Our Version in Present Day to Assure you
a Successful Blind Date: lost & found poem

A Sears Virtual Technician may text or call you
to discuss the issue with your appliance. Responding
will allow your Technician to have what is needed to
make a successful repair on the 1st trip to your home.

Your Sears service is scheduled for 6/12 8:00AM-5:00PM.
Details: https://hsn.social/vsXa5d. Text STOP
to be removed from future service updates

27

after feeling totally wasted & drained with existence
i love going to places where you can just buy things
in bulk, while think there's really something to be
said about that—to find someone loyal & reliable
& can trust in the class/ification of the homosapien
or what they conveniently refer to as the human being

28

boxes of *ramada noodles* matches mouthwash & bars of *ivory soap*
as she once unconditionally loved you like some book of coupons
meant to instantly heal all problems & everything-must-go loss

29

rows & rows & rows of roses like rebirth & redemption
like that dimly-lit malaysian restaurant looking over all
of downtown manhattan & can do no wrong & got a
whole life ahead of you while romance long-lasting
until runs up against the challenges of living &
have to decide how willing you are to keep the
flame burning in the do or die mirage of reality

30

your head hanging heavy
against the belly of some
saintly stunning dominican
daughter in her one piece
black bathing suit & long
flowing hair at the pitt st. pool
while her mom keeps an eye out
on all the drug dealers & hustlers
as we're all waiting for older brother
to return from upstate as indicated by
sheet draped from fire escape on this
warm lower east side summer's day

A Guide to that Child Hood Game Freeze Tag

when we were kids
    used to say some
           pretty deep
                crazy shit
  like if we ever get rich
       & made a million
              would purchase
one of those great big
      blushing red brick

                              brownstones
                                    on the edge of town
                                          way out in
                                                the west west village
             (not too far
                    from the meat market
                              where could smell
                                          all those freshly
                              made bagels & bialys
                                          bleary-eyed
                                                at dawn)
        jane st.
              horatio
                          where they finally
                                    leave you the hell alone

        welcoming all those
                beautiful blessed seasons
                            of such miraculous
                                      transcendent
                                                silence & stillness
              while back then
                          would have done
                                    anything for anyone
   (drag queens
          & hasidim
                    swept in a heap
                          of rags to the curb
                                          when the church
                                                      bells
                                                & foghorns
                                      go down
                                over the river)
          dropdead
                drunken
                      in one of
                            those

                    skyblue
                            subterranean
                                    publikschool
                                            gymnasiums
        where all
                your leftover
                        wiseass
                                delinquent
                                        friends
                                                        shorty
                                                    & psycho
                                                from daze
                                                    of freezetag
                                    mumble punchlines
                                        from all those
                                                sticks&stones
                                                        thrown
                        finally wailing
                                all that wizzdumb
                                        somewhere between
                                                the final bow
                                                        & original blow
                                you realize
                                        in the end
                                            is your
                                                only home

Footnote:

i haven't been back to new york for so long

and suppose the only thing i really miss are

those warm dimly-lit bookstores in the fall

those soup buns at *shanghai joes*

the succulent duck at *wing wongs*

where your fellow madman paul meyers

who worked at *soho books* when lunchbreak

came crashed through the doors and flew down

the cobblestone declaring "a fling with the wing!"

pumpkin ravioli on greene street

in soho during the holidays

A Footnote to a Footnote:

i have this guidebook for tunisia
i have never touched when i used
to work at *soho books* on west broadway
in new york & me & my boss used to go
at it back & forth at the end of the week as would
sell them to me for half price & all the employees
would just gather around & crack up hysterically as
we'd go at each other like one of those infamous arab
markets—i miss that dude paul valuzzi a half irish half
italian from the island & one day gotta get out to tunisia

31

foghorns coming around the corner
along with the old timers dragging
their *radioflyers* full of *budweiser*
down winter wonderland streets
of snow like some sort of distorted
pot of gold at the end of the rainbow
empty & hollow no longer playing

the role of king but town idiot
& pathetic jester whose wife
has lost all respect for him

32

a

those mean-spirited & malicious nurses no longer
with an ounce of calm/passion just looking to get
their pension now with potty mouths not giving
a crap who they're insulting—a matter of fact
resent their patients like young female radiologist
now turned dope addict (cuz the world just finally
got the better of her) just looking for someone to
protect her & a weekend pass during christmas
with a couple doses of liquid methadone to go
along with some man (even if some ex-con)
who gives the impression like he might
actually care or give a damn about her

b

the mountain boys used to say such stuff
like after you woke up were like crazy
for 15 minutes or so & took that long to
recover or get back to normal. never quite
understood that but always sounded pretty
damn deep & profound & think am starting
to understand that now—why were some of
the nicest & kindest & most down-to-earth guys
you'd ever want to know & why probably were
always addicted to some sort of liquor or drug
—at the change of seasons you see all those
madmen out of nowhere just suddenly wandering
past your window as if coming out of hibernation

the pretty girls in their mountainclimbing shorts
& pigtails with toddlers found returning
back to porches from faraway oceans

c

why every freakin time seems
like yer being a mensch or doing
a mitzvah (yiddish translation good
deed doing your due diligence) that
horrible awful obvious repetitive
bureaucracy comes back to bite
you & kick you in the head (ie
getting stuck down in stifling
subway ny transit system &
big brother comes on over
the speakers "thank you for
your patience . . . thank you for
your patience" & wanna just
put a bullet in your head)
tell the wife rather be dead
the difference between feeling
cursed & blessed—tell her again
be nice if once just once some mad
wild friend from your adolescence
with mad heart & soul just called up
& left some good ole spirited message
like they used to "hey joe, where ya goin
with that gun in your hand . . ." (hendrix)

Around 12 Reasons Not To Take Your Life

you wake up to *the ed sullivan show*
& a very young tony bennett
with those nice kind deep blue
tearful eyes looking up to the sky

you see that bleak sun breaking through
the blinds like eggs overeasy at some boxcar diner
you ask your son what he fell asleep to & tells you
bruce springsteen & you find yourself remembering
& singing every last single word to "thunder road"
you find yourself as a child in kindergarten doing
a play on the revolutionary war & the first one to
die which was a black man "who was the first to
shed his blood? crispus attucks! crispus attucks!"
you find yourself peddling your tricycle down the aisle
of a packed-filled auditorium with a girl on the back
& whole class singing "the handsome prince
came riding by! riding by! riding by!"
you find yourself walking down the aisle
& eventually taking her all around the world
you think about your kid who you
sincerely love more than life itself
you see the black & white *eve arden show* & wonder
if back then also liked being eaten out & spreading open
those long wishbone legs & going down on that stuffing
you see after the first serious snow melting the seasonal
tradition of that river overflowing heading to spring
you think of all those things you gotta get to
your apple orchard similar to robert frost's
who tried to plant 100 & never quite could
your black currant & gooseberry bushes
your brussel sprouts to be harvested

description of project . . .

wondering if your company can actually
put up a nice deep dense forest for us
maybe one of those babbling brooks
running through it for purposes of peace
& quiet & solitude & escapism & those
holy & sacred claps of thunder before

it all comes down & rescues & saves us
with birch & beech trees & a whole mess
of sugar maples if so choose to get a hankering
hanging buckets for thick buckwheat pancakes

Premise #1

when you hear wood creaking
whether it's in the tall distant
whispering trees of the lagoon
or that french antique table contracting
and expanding at the change of seasons
you at last know the truths of the universe

Premise #2

the essence of truth (along with its selfsame
images of dreaming and multiple experiences
of surreal virtue) will always break through
all the bullshit rhetoric of non-truth(s)

Premise #3

the truest philosophical proclamations
is when taking it out of context, putting
it back in, and removing it again; all types
of emotion, past experiences, resemblances
and any possible moral & ethical consequences

Premise #4

the absurdity of such linguistic statements
like "let's get everything back to normal"

which always seemed to more so have some
thing of a paradoxical, overwhelming effect

Premise #5

growing up those perfectly triangular
homes along the side of the highway
always loved—guess it was their simplicity
and geometry, nothingness and anonymity
moving from one empty space to the other

Premise #6

the developers show up clearing out
that part of the dense rainforest putting
up their white highrise monochromatic
condominiums for the pasty caucasians
looking to make an investment, purchase
units & gobble up the pristine virginal area.
included with this blueprint for an efficient
oasis is a big blue pool, pina-coladas, native
species, native senoritas, championship 18 hole
golf course & a whole squadron of golf carts—
iguanas & sandpipers scuttling for shelter . . .

Premise #7

love these days
    how they have like
        these contests
            for writing
      requesting like 'decentered
          or marginalized' voices
              or whatever those
                  big political correct
                      bullshit words are

   once again
charge you
      like 35 dollars
       like in 1972
  when you saw
     on the back
      of some
        superhero comic
   one of those ads
      for *charles atlas*
       just to mail
        off a dollar
so that beach bully
   would no longer
      kick sand in your face
        & you enthusiastically
          stuck a buck
           in an envelope
      & never heard back
        from them

Premise #8

with women
  it always seems
     2 b
      the tiny details
        & small stuff
  like having nowhere
     2 go
      after a bad breakup
& her taking u
   inn in
     the stifling summer
       midnight of manhattan
  & making u tuna
with cilantro

(the "planet of the apes"
muted on television)
telling her joking around
could love her forever . . .

Premise #9

if only the actual infamous 'court of law' had more
sincere defense attorneys & prosecutors who seem
to come across more so as unconvincing actors
the prejudicial judge with his drinking habit
while appears they all care more about
the process procedure protocol & presentation
than having anything to do with guilt or innocence

Premise #10

the secrets of advertising
or philosophy more accurately
the exploration of perverse evil virtues

A Pain Diary:

✿

it's not so much really depressed
it's just when surrounded
by so many idiots kinda
hard to get out of it . . .

✿

why does it always seem the ones you go all out for
are the exact ones in the long-run who betray you?

❂

people are enough to drive you mad
don't try to figure them out as in fact
without a doubt will make you take it out
on yourself don't pass go don't collect 200

❂

in truth they never get back to you
what they exactly told & promised you
appearing like the opposite of god, jesus

heard they got graffiti
scribbled all over
plymouth rock

❂

we are all but the remains of
beat-up broken hearts & souls
no need to go digging for bones
there is a spirit out there and can
feel it on the cobblestone & shore

❂

living in one of those bizarre foreign
monochromatic suburban homeowners
associations where everyone's always
competitively one-upping each other
but never speak to one another is
like one of those strange religions
(with their man-made issues and
conflicts) for all the wrong reasons

❄

deep in the heart of the suburbs they collect
their shiny objects and pop out their quota
of kids but what's the difference and distinction
cause both get treated like possessions and end
up feeling this raw desperate nihilistic feeling of
dread and pure emptiness having lost all touch
with their identity and reason for living when
leaving the house in the pitch-black darkness
of the morning and returning in the evening
(as if some existential crime has been committed)
going through the motions like some slave-zombie
for the wife children and mortgage just to keep
the whole half-crazed absurd illusion going

❄

suburbia takes on certain absurd
delusional forms of 'slavery' with
one's idealized vision this is what
happiness is but once experience
the mentality (and character and
behavior) of the neighbor feel
[deep empty hollow pangs of]
existentially betrayed and cheated

❄

suburbia will be the death of you
unless in fact it's already happened
whereas in this illusion who'd even notice?

❄

all those things that make one 'rich & famous'
is the exact dynamic to being self-destructive
(making the mind mundane & monotonous

sacrificing a whole life just trying to keep up
& maintain living the half-crazed "illusion")
like the nature & life & times of the drug
addict just feening for that fix & spending
a whole life & existence having to do all
that criminal shit just to become content

❀

rich people (or that whole classless class
of wannabes) never ever seem quite satisfied
and always bothered (higher than holy & hostile)
trying to act like you're the cause to all their problems

they take way too 'seriously' literal and obvious that proverb
'a sacrifice to the gods'—the sexless wife tortures some poor
boy just trying to do his summer job "is that made out of lard!?"

❀

growing up you had this fellow delinquent pal
who i guess was considered one of those bad boys
from south america and of course all the girls wanted
him and whenever you hung out with him he and his
brother always playfully harassing the housekeeper
saying dirty things in spanish—man looking back
things were so crazy back then and from what i heard
became one of those real driven successful businessmen

❀

back then lost so many of my friends to cocaine
as supposedly that's what it meant to fit in & be
a part of the mainstream & didn't seem particularly
original or creative & think probably even felt so hurt
& betrayed couldn't even begin to fathom why they'd
go that way while so out of touch with my feelings;
parents just moving us out to these strange & silent

'growing up absurd' suburbs whereas those kids did
absolutely nothing to earn it with workaholic parents
who ironically were like world-renowned neurologists
& attorneys with practices in multiple cities like nyc &
palm springs & in the movie industry & guess just learned to
accept it like this was the nature of the culture & community
i lived in & just the way things were & was so young & not
yet cognitively or intellectually mature probably not even
aware feeling so lonely & alienated (or maybe deep down
inside like somehow i deserved it) while subconsciously
might make something far better of myself as just get in
parents stationwagon with my downtime like some
kind of secret mission (& act of independence) &
anonymously head down the avenue when those
cafe latte *barnes & nobles* chain bookstores first
started opening & pick up books for extra reading
the biggest ones i could possibly read mostly by like
sartre & pound & proust & dostoevsky who also too
seemed profoundly spiritually dead & strangely estranged
in their own ways & be just like them & try to be as smart
as i could be sublimating all those really hurt & damaged
feelings with my own far more intelligent intimate revenge

❁

friends for no particular reason go missing-in-action
which almost seems close to that of being a sin . . .

❁

we end up eventually chasing former ghosts of ourselves

❁

my theory with the institute of marriage
is we end up haphazardly becoming
one of those amorphous specimens
stored safely in a jar of formaldehyde

the stain remover guy
arrives and charming wife
greets him with a how's life?

☼

they bring in the analysts
for the football game
for the assassination
trained elephants are
led into the circus tent

☼

why is it always hypocrites passing all that judgment
while like one of those infamous word problems from
adolescence like to just casually push them out a moving
vehicle (doing 60) subtracting "to be or not to be" from
"i think therefore i am" to try and figure out the exact
determination/destination of a 'life of leisure,' comfortable
living, everyday functioning, contemplation and contentment

☼

it is my estimation that we learn the most in elementary
during such periods like recess when kids collectively go
crashing through doors to the schoolyard dividing up into
natural subgroups of gender and sexuality and sensibility
and aesthetics and athletic prowess and traditional passed
down games of imagination (developing a certain sense of
autonomy and self-determination) making connections with
similar-like character and behaviors (pleasant repetitive
routines & rituals) congregating for instinctive purposes
of socialization and asserting one's identity (dreams,
fantasies) state of being and inevitable personality

✺

man people will try to fuck with your paradise
until you feel like some kinda sacrifice

you plan trips on *expedia*
to solve that fight or flight syndrome . . .

✺

a shame how higher education in amerika
is just wasted on the very privileged & entitled
& those who could not possibly appreciate or be grateful

✺

why is it those who are so often deemed "difficult"
when you meet them bare absolutely no resemblance
to this description and just present as a bit defensive
due to a whole hell of a lot of damage and experience

✺

family dysfunction is a form of literal clinical 'role-reversal'
along with disinformation, miscommunication, scapegoating
and gaslighting whose deep and profound fragile triggers
lead to retraumatization and self-fulfilling prophecies

✺

i have always developed this strange sense of confidence
and will to move on when not been around "mankind."
whenever they opened their pieholes and talked
all this asinine shit (and all those lies) is when i
not by coincidence questioned & doubted my life

❊

all those men claimed had this great reputation
when you met them my first reaction always
was are these the ones you're talking about?

❊

how come all those confident people
they always talk about some of the most
boring obvious arrogant assholes but those
lacking in it seem to have so much more to offer

❊

the very few who devote their lives to being positive & productive
cannot even fathom the mentality of those being petty & vindictive

❊

phonies are pretty much the exact same people
it's just where they decide to be detail-oriented

❊

we have a moral and value system
in so much as we choose to have
one.or for that matter ever use it

these people can get awfully tricky
(in their presentation) and what
works subtly to their advantage

❊

for every great poet & philosopher
it is good to be doubted (questioned
and interrogated) by those they know

couldn't even begin to understand them

☼

it is more than ironic that often those sometimes
advocating for peace seem awfully [just as] passive
aggressive, self-righteous, controlling and alienating

☼

we live in a culture of clueless know-it-all idiots
aloof & arrogant who have memorized their list
of political-correct acronyms, yet whenever it
comes down to the nitty-gritty have absolutely
no idea about sympathy (spirit) morals or ethics

☼

they're so much anarchists
(these so-called presses)
they can't even get back to you
that seems more arrogant & aloof

☼

wisdom is just getting through all the
bullshit & lies to figure out what's right

☼

if so busy just trying to maintain
when are you gonna step out to get
a little taste of that paradise you've
been so desperately trying to attain

❀

why is it those citizens (not the veterans)
who always have these really strong patriotic
opinions about america never left its borders?

❀

we have this obsessive need to
travel and visit different tourist sites
what a bizarre dynamic and notion

why not just sit on park benches
and smell the roses, children, young
women seductively doing their rounds

the marching band
flamenco dancers
return to the ghetto

❀

'the tourist' always constantly talking about culture
makes me sick to the stomach as if it's some kind of
exclusive competition or trying desperately to one-up
or some sort of "exceptionalism" and if for some crazy
reason you decide to show up not always quite as receptive
and welcoming, while ironically treating you like 'a stranger'
trying way too hard to alienate and prove you're not on their level

❀

i have often found it close to criminal
those who have deliberately made
you doubt and question yourself
coming from an insecure, passive
aggressive, mean-spirited, jealous
and envious place almost shakespearean

speaking from both sides of their mouths
(anna freud refers to this in her defense
mechanisms as 'reaction-formation' when
flattering with proclamations but really meaning
the exact opposite) in how they try to take you out

❊

the compulsive liar is always never 'quite right'

❊

all that bullshit and flattery and gaslighting
and taking you for granted—man how they wear
you down and force you to become a man of wisdom

❊

i'm that cat who keeps on fighting myself out the corner
running into a brand new challenger who keeps on just
hitting me with the exact same punches until i just become
bored and indifferent and immune to it all and take home
that pretty seductive girl who shows off the round cards
and after you finally win her favor enter a whole other
arena and power-struggle and form of domestic violence
constantly on the defensive not even sure anymore her
purpose why she got into it trying to win by no decision

❊

i remember that job delivering controlled substances
in lockboxes with that old timer through the midnight
mountains of vermont to the old age homes and juvenile
centers as he suddenly posed the question "why do you
think women are so much better looking these days?" and
me instantly just coming up with "think maybe they're just
going more to the healthclub and not wearing as much makeup
going back to a more simple spare beauty" while he just sat

there in silence as if tacitly agreeing as we started to rummage
in the back of the truck for a couple those brown paper bags
and carry it up the elevator to that young ivory girl nurse who
worked the nightshift we both had apparently fallen in love with

✺

is there a news team
that will tell you about
"heartbreaking conditions"
on a cognitive & behavioral
level where out in the country
they'll eventually get to
& in the city not
quite exactly

✺

working art's movie theater
on 57th st. in manhattan
that documentary about
thelonious monk and
some survivor living
in brooklyn after the
concentration camps
you residing the last
stop stillwell avenue
all the way at the end
of the boardwalk
in coney island
pulling your shades
down hearing the
hypnotic rhythm
of the ocean
dozing off

☼

erica got very mad at me today. told me how much
she hated me using the word "hankering" and how i
needed to stop. i told her i liked it and was just fooling
around and being playful. she angrily retorted how much
it pissed her off while i defended myself how i was simply
coming from a good place and enjoyed using southern
slang, as guess that's just the thing about the institution
of marriage—how every time you think you're being this
good guy they're accusing you of some kinda petty crime

☼

wife rushing around the home
doing her daily chores tells you
in her cute adorable demure voice
how something was an honest mistake

i naturally respond about the irony or
double-entendre how if you linguistically
deconstruct it from a wittgenstein point of view

her being a girl from the bronx
snaps back you're an honest mistake

☼

when you marry a simple sweet girl
you end up sacrificing & devoting your
life (whether you like it or not) to her

☼

freud in his own subtle brilliant way helped us to get it all out
of our system and face our fears and phobias and neuroses
and abnormal way of thinking and eventually functioning
and for that we should be eternally grateful as opposed

to being critical about his methodology and how he went
about doing it—i'll take that any day as opposed to how
you are required and mandated to write papers these days
with all this obvious and boring empirical reporting and notating
(just to prove your theory or thesis which "can" be manipulated)
while ironically get very little out of it as feels more how you are
supposed to present a psychological paper as opposed to any
real new true significant thoughts and ideas on the subject

✿

those things which give us melancholia
they say that term's outdated but i'm
not so sure? (yer gonna tell me freud &
shakespeare & all those ole playwrights?)
as feels perfectly apropos like one of those
classic onomatopoeias & the result of people
who consistently don't return calls with wife
driving you up the wall—the best thing about
childhood & seemed to redeem it all was tuna
fish & matzoh the next day in the cafeteria . . .

✿

remember to dream
why whenever we
order chinese
we always
have the need
to speak oppositely
like "i'll get a chicken wing"
you drive through the purple
shutters at dusk to pick up. . .

❉

"come-on! let's get serious!"
what exactly would that entail
and what a ridiculous statement

❉

i always found it funny how far off
people's perception of me was like
some punchline without the riddle
or do i have that backwards?

❉

why do all those expressions
always say such shit like
i'd follow him into battle
or the ends of the earth while
why not just *vasack's drinking
tavern* where the old timers at
the bar are getting handjobs from
the cute girls from the neighborhood

❉

those during those weird and strange interludes
for such things like interviews who used to make
instant bold claims like "i'm a people person"
i always felt an instant disdain even a little
bit turned-off slightly alienated and afraid
wondering what were the other options?

❉

those who claim certain generations
also seem just slightly abandoned
(a rationalization) overcompensating

not quite believing their own conviction

✽

those who make such declarative statements
or proclamations like "trust me" "believe me"
or "i mean what i say and say what i mean"
always seem just a little lacking in identity

✽

it is usually the repetitive, linguistic pattern
(its natural form and structure of 'a few choice
words' along with phonetic triggers) which more
so allows you to intuitively, empirically understand
the sentence (and emotion) over having anything to
do with true substance (or the nature of the thought
and idea). similarly, reverse-engineering, deconstruction
of saying absolutely nothing at all pretty much says it all

✽

context only contains context
once we address it as context
things hold very little meaning
without context and thus it would
be fair to conclude that life holds
very little true meaning without these
specific considerations and selfsame efforts

✽

the critic way too sweeping cerebral confident
in his comments while feels like never had
love (or for that matter good sex) before

☼

culture & civilization just seems
like some silly reenactment of
really poor character & behavior

☼

a postmodern dream from very long ago—
driving down some long empty white sandy road
(in cairo) seeing both the golden arches & pyramids
whose forms & images just naturally blended together
neither one seeming more particularly holy or sacred which
in fact made the whole scene more believable, transcendent

☼

it's those thematic nightmares in our childhood
not by coincidence which haunt us in our later
years and not quite (those self same traits and
characteristics) all our dreams [not] come true

☼

"the idiots" waste way too much time
in their lives self-advocating idealizing
and commercializing who they are
by obsessively flying their flags

☼

what do we have to live for?
well when you break it down
probably not too much at all
while think far more accurate
all those things that we don't

❀

paranoia seems like all you got left
after reality proves not to give a shit

you take a trip with wife to panama
city, florida knowing nothing about it

you heard the mexican drug cartel
has started to infestate the resorts

i guess the government
no longer paying them off

❀

fantasy just as important as anything
going on in waking reality as more
often than not leads to great things
[expansion] of the mind and being

❀

those good intimate relationships
like sleepovers that never end . . .

❀

you can sometimes learn more from a one-night stand
than you do in a whole lifetime feeling like a new man
taking that early morning subway back from manhattan
redeemed and reborn to your brownstone in brooklyn

❀

almost all the girls i grew up with seemed to care
more about their reflection in the mirror making
it virtually impossible and futile to compete with

❄

lust (and sex) *is* a form of love
considering how it instantly heals on an
emotional psychological spiritual even chemical level

❄

all man cares—to rest head
on woman's breast to hear
that echoing tick-tock
to prove he still exists

❄

you become something of a criminal & comedian
after many years of marriage *wanted* dead or alive

❄

true love is having the ability to read between
the lines all those things they try to do for you

❄

i have gone on interviews where i was perfectly dressed to
the t with sincerely absolutely no experience for the position
required, and while the interviewer respectfully showed me
around the work area and all those little neurotic employees
doing their due diligence darting in and out of their cubicles
just naturally noticed and observed with their non-verbals
and body language how they were all just so damn defensive,
fragile, insecure, jealous and even hostile (as if i was the one
who was going to take away their job) and thought in the back
of my mind, man even if by some stroke of luck or miracle
this person happened to offer me the position sure
as heck didn't wanna have anything to do with it

☼

those bosses i look back at with the most fondness
were those who were just as hard-working & diligent
may have even had something like serious drinking habits
but knew always had your back (and for all these exact
reasons loved working for them) while ironically found these
same traits & characteristics with women i've known in my past

☼

did god ever have a savior complex?
think about that one when every so
often have the need to turn to him
for purposes of support & guidance

☼

those who play god are 'so far' from
it, while ironically the exact opposite
of those selfsame traits & characteristics

☼

has anyone ever convicted the masses?

☼

the real sign of a working functioning democracy
are all those things we take for granted and if
remain complacent the exact thing that kills it

☼

these days everyone seems to conveniently safely
be hiding behind their systems and protocols with
little to no accountability at all affecting the overall
collective-unconscious and the 'growth and development'

of human character or lack there of which seems something
of a bit of a pathetic tragic loss of intimacy (individually and
in the social-cultural landscape) when you think about it but
ironically that there lies the real crux of the problem cause
no one seems to truly care enough to really think about it

❀

what a bunch of bizarre oxy/morons
how humans appear more broken
fragmented and incomplete when
they supposedly grow up (mature)

and the closer you get to them when
honestly couldn't really give a damn

boy how these 'little men' sure
know how to flatter themselves

❀

all these people with the need
to be flying their flags with such
prim & proper pomp & circumstance
advertising, commercializing their false pride
don't seem to have a hell of alot going on in their lives

❀

you're simply mortal
they don't return calls
(law of transitivity)
all telemarketers!

❅

ghosts creep in when we can no longer
fool ourselves with the rhetoric and
rationalizations we refer to as
this thing called living

❅

if decide to become a drunk
best to do so in later life
with not too much to
look forward to

& so much to
look back on

❅

camus in his philosophy talks alot about
the topic of suicide but the way i look at it
is any of this life really worth it? i remember
this ridiculous image of some author just
looking all despondent and down in the
dumps just sitting there for his book signing
and pretty much no one showing up like jesus'
last supper without any of the apostles to know
that all of humanity and human nature pretty
much takes on a certain form of betrayal

❅

people will try to make you hate yourself—
i forgot about those people some time ago
cause are neither people (nor honestly
ever display any true sense of self)

✻

keep a close eye out on your own self-worth
as will try and pull you down into their hell

✻

i remember at a very young age always feeling confused
by friends who never followed through—matter of fact
think may have even experienced a sense of disbelief
and feeling deep pangs of desertion without being
aware of it—that kids at such a young age could
be so indifferent and full of it, and most likely why
i may have become 'wild' and oppositional-defiant
—how wisdom eventually becomes scoping these
similar behavioral patterns and selfsame traits and
characteristics in strangers, peers and acquaintances
and finding just that one rare and unique individual
who can be consistently trusted and believed in

✻

that kid i used to work with out in providence
pretty much deserted and abandoned by his
mom and dad and mom who met a new man
and chose him over him and ended up in the
shelters out of a hell of alot of pain and suffering
and acting-out and couldn't stay out of trouble
taking on a volunteer job at the horse stables
where it was his chore to groom all the horses
and proved to be so caring and compassionate
as well as made a real connection with all those
young male and female cops who ironically turned
out far more nurturing, relatable, and sympathetic

❈

maybe it wasn't just all that simplistic
patronizing psych.101 of 'acting-out'
and 'reaching out for help' but spiritually
emotionally needing to just get it all out
for necessary purposes of identity & self

❈

those who rarely ever speak the truth
(by linguistic and mathematical rules)
cannot ever possibly be honest people

❈

why is it that 'the innocent' (in demeanor)
are the ones who ironically always end
up feeling excruciatingly guilty?

❈

freud speaks quite eloquently and goes into great depth
about the profound primitive conflict of enmeshment
and triangulation in father-son relationships in his
"oedipus complex" but feel so much more can be said
about the role of the "wife-mother" and her 'abnormal'
acting-out when feeling emotionally and spiritually
subjugated and neglected by her husband [transferring
that lack of intimacy, affection and attention] taking it out
on her son (sometimes not even aware of it) in a bizarre
form of attraction, munchausen-like 'reactive-formation'
often active, impulsive effort towards 'embarrassing and
humiliation' and hostile and passive-aggressive behavior

✺

can a daughter catch munchausen from her mother?

✺

if people were only as fair and logical as their emotionality
erratic, impulsive [in]ability to be hostile and temperamental

✺

those who we are constantly seeking approval
(like some cycle of abuse) ironically seem
like the ones who never get back to you

✺

i just 'can't help but to feel' we're all
just like these broken damaged souls
with hooks through our jaws constantly
getting betrayed and caught by these
soulless motherfuckers out for blood
somehow through a hell of alot of
suffering and struggling getting away
and figuring out their patterns through
a certain sort of reverse-engineering and
this sadly enough is what gives us our wisdom

✺

faith one of the hardest things to keep
when surrounded by so many thieves
who don't give a damn about a thing

❋

the thing about pettiness is you can never quite get
to the bottom of it as so low down beyond recognition

❋

people will try to break you with their cryptic statements

❋

often the subtlest of liars the biggest betrayer

❋

if only the lengths that people go to hold grudges
was as long as the same effort to show how
much they in reality actually admire them

❋

people just don't listen which feels a little abusive

❋

even the church people can't give you a straight answer

❋

one of the greatest crimes
a crime of passion as
has to do with life
while everything
else practically
the opposite

☼

the one thing man seems consistent with
is all the lies and bullshit—that tradition
where they're socially late and when
they show up just want then outta
your fucken home; funny when
i woke up this morning
was in a pretty good mood . . .

☼

it's so difficult choosing your battles
when they're shooting and coming
at you from every which direction

first you got self-defense
which is your integrity and
honor and morals and ethics

then your sanity and self-preservation
and if got any leftover a little vacation

☼

during that courting honeymoon period
it's so damn romantic and escapist we
have 'practically' no time to realistically
reflect or look forward to the future—why
would we? this the most keen & perfect time
to forgive & forget everything which preceded it

☼

there should be a suicide hallmark card
just couldn't deal anymore with all
the dumbmestik bullshit no mo

a sale on lobster rolls at *hannaford*

✿

the one thing i really like living in the mountains
in small town amerika is on the news they list
all the petty criminals and their ages and feel
like really get to know the population better
—school closings due to bat inspections
interviewing that proud old lady who owns
a pizzeria in that barren bordertown and that
pretty young newscaster like some monalisa
with thick eyebrows and a little too much makeup on
who tells us about genocide and natural catastrophes
then instantly starts smiling moving on to the weather

✿

seen so many women turn guys to drinking
and thought if they only turned away
from them and towards living

✿

have suffered survived all those wild wicked winds
most likely having become one of those ghost-phantoms
devoid of emotion but perhaps in fact that much more introspective
philosophical and spiritual, amorphous, animated, distinct and lucid

✿

it's funny in this life you always seem
to get misinterpreted (the most) by the
little people who couldn't possibly know
a single thing about you (most of all themselves)

☼

people use vocabulary or specific words
(and make assertions) not by coincidence
for things they are more accurately guilty
of almost as an extension to their subconscious

☼

"politically correct" two words i detest the most
in the english language ('political' and 'correct'
which describe and tell you absolutely nothing)
and when you're done with these people always
left with this 'indescribable' profound feeling
of [in]complete loneliness and emptiness

☼

we feel most empty around those
who are supposed to play the role
of substance, depth and meaning

☼

asking someone to validate is like explaining
a punchline which has a real pathetic quality
putting you in a pretty damn lonely place like
some kind of proverbial solitary confinement

☼

watch out! that person you may think
a thief or criminalized when you meet
him one of the most honest and nicest
of guys—a whole family of absurd
frightened delusional tourists stuffed
in their climate-controlled locked-down car
delivered straight from the dead end to the mall

✻

even your fucken tree guy won't get back to you
or return emails or voicemail says all filled up
with messages and only gets back to you at
his own convenience and when it works to
his advantage and you think damn gotta
deal with this even from my goddamn
arborist when you're just simply trying
to make your property look adequate
while is this not the classic oxymoronic
linguistic breakdown of "human nature"

✻

looking back the only one i recall
i ever really trusted was my painting
boss who seemed like he really cared
or gave a damn or could talk to or listened
—was one of those really brave motherfuckers
who was a paratrooper during the war and wild
at heart and if you worked hard and showed up
which i always did didn't know any different
would pay you at week's end under the table
while at the end of a job would like polish
off a couple cases in some old lady's basement
and somehow stagger home trying to make it back
in one piece—boy he sure loved to tie one on but
looking back one of the only ones i ever remember
really trusting with a damn fine heart and soul. . .

✻

my heroes growing up
those glossy posters
stuck to my wall of
bob mcadoo
spencer haywood

walt "clyde" frazier
earl "the pearl" monroe
do they make them humble
anymore like barry sanders
when he scored a touchdown
and looked for a referee
just to hand the ball to

☼

i know this may sound cliche
and probably already been
said many times before
but those classic old
signs "most wanted"
more than likely
people who
deep down
inside (stigmatized
criminalized) never
felt very 'wanted'
most of their lives

☼

why is it you end up feeling so much more alone
around those so-called goody-goody good deed
doers as opposed to maybe chatting with some ex-con
or spending quality time with your dog sitting nobly by your side?

☼

it is true we end up feeling so [much more] lonely
when we are around those who are supposed to
present (for purposes of meaning and being
and functioning) as us feeling less lonely

❧

there should be a disorder where people
just keep on making you feel lonelier and
lonelier although i ain't so sure that's so
much a disorder as more so a pattern
of self-involved, stubborn, know-it-all
motherfuckers i more so prefer my dog
riding shotgun on the way to the dump

❧

does everyone
have a talk show
and is everyone a star?
feels like everyone's got
warhol's 15 minutes of fame
like old wilted flowers in a vase

❧

seems like everyone's a "best-selling"
author these days promoting their book
—looks more like that crooked slutty
aunt from columbus ohio who tried
to seduce you over the holidays

❧

most family dysfunction
is like those board games
only a couple leftover broken
pieces and lost the directions

❁

all those things that we fixate or obsess over
more so often a substitute (spiritual transitional
object of 'high-expressed emotion') for all those
things that got suddenly profoundly lost and taken
from us a very long time ago; this is why the physical
and emotional act and dynamic of love and romance
does such a good job in instantly healing [that self
same "illusion"] all that unnecessary perseverating

❁

it's so difficult to remember any of those
people places or things which are corrupt
as think most likely psychologically block
(it) due to reasons traumatic or just so damn
petty and pathetic empirically not even worth it

❁

man does himself a grave disservice when forgets
about his moral & ethical reflection & revelations
whilst with this repetition ends up in a "living hell"

❁

when all else 'fails' man turns to superstition

❁

guilt more often than not is a 'substitute'
or overcompensation for all those things
deeper primitive conflicted and anguished

☼

sometimes the mind (with all those stressors and anxiety)
just does not process the right way and may even possibly
reach the wrong conclusions while it does help every so often
to try and consider the nature and physiological patterns of the
caterpillar in its cocoon (with absolutely no doubt or question to
how it reached its truths) just naturally metamorphosing and flying away

☼

faith is all that's leftover when can't catch a break
on off off off broadway—that rent-controlled flat for
$325 a month between riverside & west end of course
with that absentee landlord who does nothing and
gotta toss a sock with a key attached through the
window for your buddies which provides that
much more meaning & memories touching
on the concept & principle of faith & being

☼

dreams—simply forms, images, structures, a medium
that we are not aware of in our conscious being
(overwhelming our reality for a number of different
reasons) but play themselves out clearly and lucidly
in our subconscious like some surreal 'reel to real'
(with people and things representing these exact
emotions and feelings) and that self same plot
and theme which appears to be troubling us
so deeply and profoundly rarely without
any ending because of course obviously a
resolution has not been [close to] reached

☼

there's a certain concrete keen spirit
in our lucid dreams that penetrate
and seeps from the cerebral membrane
and if we are receptive and aware enough
during the day spiritually awakens our waking
being and even temporarily heals and saves us

☼

those dreams of fantasy and when you
are asleep are what dreams are made
of and the things that save you . . .

☼

traveling heals practically everything
(more accurately when reminiscing)
but usually somewhere about half
way in you always find yourself
with this deep empty hollow
feeling brooding about your
mortality and wanting to just
go right back to where it all began
think the buddhists were right about
all that suffering and the reason why
the ancient egyptians turned to reincarnation
you hear this british man hollering at his kid "stop
winching!" and think you know exactly what that means

☼

i weep
when i think
about my memories

of paris
of paradise
which i imagine

can no longer be
is that the thing
about old age?

❧

old age something like
a depressed new england town
when the prostitutes come out at night
and leftover bottle of moonshine
chilling in the refrigerator...

❧

we seem so much more fragile & vulnerable
when we grow older while as a "wild child"
so much more resilient with the exact same stuff
which just bounces right off us—playing hoop
after school taking in all those stray ethereal scents
of the seasons and all those rivers running through

we count down days to spring
when *dairy cream* opens

❧

the imagination just tries to sift & strain
all that pain from all that suffering that
shouldn't have happened in the first place

❅

i hope with the afterlife it just turns out like those nice
young kind secretaries you can make small talk with

after that it's completely beyond
my reach out of my *jury's diction*

❅

in the morning the mist comes in
over the mountain and wraps itself
around the trees up on top as if forming
their own private pagodas there's nothing
left to live for and that means the world. . .

❅

falling in love with girl selling roses on the way to my funeral
inside my mausoleum they sell souvenir plates for a steal
you fantasize about all those girls not very good for you

❅

you found you learned so much more
from all those crazy girls who
had nothing left to live for

❅

with the magician and his pretty assistant
through the secret psychological act of
'transference' really just wants to make
his wife vanish in thin air getting replaced
by this simple silent vision who will just
finally at last listen and believe in him

✤

those yellow brick brownstones
along the boardwalk in brighton
playing handball all day on the ocean

yeah it was survival—hoping in the back
of my mind those days might last forever

✤

mom gave birth
to a radio show
host when the rain
came down like
drizzle in coney
island pulling
your shade
down from
your grave
yard shift
trying to
get in a
couple
good
winks
of
shut
eye
taught
to never
give up
big boys
don't cry
and to be
persistent
on your
filthy futon

on the floor
in the last
room at
the end
of the
world

☼

dracula sipping at his iced coffee
in the early dawn, numb like his
pal frank who got hit by a truck
never quite the same and now
casually sleepwalking with
a cognitive delay neither
here nor there living
happily ever after with
his mom in the carroll
gardens section
of brooklyn

all's good as life
highly overrated

☼

living in a culture of social media where everybody's famous
(for 15 minutes) has a bit of an anticlimactic ridiculous and
absurd quality to it. i remember as a social worker picking
up my client for his session at the mental health clinic and
him telling me how they were all so excited as his stepfather
that night was playing in some sort of gig on *youtube* and
sincerely didn't know about any of those types of things
nor what to make of it while i guess all i could do was
give them my most hearty and healthiest of wishes

❀

we spend our whole existence just trying
to find and capture beauty and happiness
and always (in something of a delusional manner)
just barely missing it (all that existential artificial
spiritual solemn silence) getting stuck in bum
dabumpa rush hour traffic in the morning and
evening returning home barely able to get
words out keeping it all in having to meet
those meaningless quotas & neverending
needs of clients & bosses & petty passive
aggressive fellow workers so far from
having anything to do with that abstract
image & vision of any beauty or happiness

❀

more times than not we get misinterpreted
and underestimated by those who really
don't know a thing about themselves
while to say it all becomes a theater of
the absurd would be a vast understatement

❀

find it kinda funny how those who have been
around the block and done their fare share
of living and suffering actually in fact turns
out some of the best listeners and say some
of the most deep and keen profound shit
(where you feel instantly understood and
validated) while those with all those licenses,
initials, and acronyms behind their names
end up feeling the most alone and alienated

✻

man becomes like some absurd ridiculous solomon
with a dollhouse burning on one shoulder & wonder
woman engulfing him on the other taking the local
everyday of his existence kafkaesquely never ever
quite reaching it or that fascinating psychological
phenomenon of 'dissociative fugue' of getting
there but not quite knowing how he did so; the
aroma of chinese & roses will keep him going

✻

suburbia or suburbanization with its monochromatic
one-upping mentality of perfectionism (practically
everything's about making 'an impression') actually
in fact alienating one from their own core being and
purpose and meaning eventually touching on all those
empty nihilistic feelings and one's own mortality ironically
(in this frequent absurd competitive imitative environment and
social landscape) making one uncomfortable in their own skin

✻

did the flowers ever get moody
when that neighbor in her pink
bathrobe & high heels used to
loosely groom them across from
the vacuum repair & funeral home?

✻

mo whacks him over skull
                    with his red hot poker
this time concussing curly
putting him in a coma
while the cop cars
& ambulances

with their flashing
sirens do their
nightly rounds
coming over
to the ole drunken
merchant marine
in his
brownstone
in brooklyn
well known
to the neighbors
for drama & drinking
the next day they act
like nothing happened
heading to confession
—see that is the thing
about the human species
having to do with all things
sadistic slapstick & ceremony

✿

if it's humor that has kept us going
through 1000's of years of persecution
must in fact be the greatest vaudevillians

✿

i need legal help from my legal help

young handsome enforcer
who all the girls are head
over heels in love with
weeps in penalty box

winnipeg always goes out first round . . .

☼

we are all but mere victims to our dreams
& die a slow death on a daily basis

man goes to vegas . . .

☼

paradise is often just simply a roll of the dice

☼

erickson in his human stages of growth & development
should have had a phase in later life where you look back
at old girlfriends like some sort of cognitive behavioral
exercise to try and get closure and make sense of life

☼

with women you have to really just
know how to read between the lines
while end up doing a heck of alot of squinting
until you're practically blind—is that where
they came up with the line blinded by love?

☼

good women make you grin
& bring out the substance
& meaning of what often
seems a dormant existence

o—the seasons!

❀

whenever i'm really down in the dumps and blue
i turn to memories of past girlfriends and all the
different sexual positions we did not necessarily
caring about my own pleasure but pleasing them
and watching them with their sexually repressed
tormented eyes closed writhing in total ecstasy
and liberated and me just watching that turning
me on and allowing me to get off and forget about
all those petty fucked-up things in life which just
get under your skin and that state of ecstasy and
pure emptiness and bliss of just forgetting it all
(all those conflicts and crises) proving to be
the greatest feeling of all time like riding your
sled as a wild boy without a care or worry in
the world cherishing the mad sacred moment
down the snowy hills of the twilight graveyard

❀

in the end we take a partner, lover, or soulmate
to try and get all the [bull]shit of life & existence
off our chest to find out at best all just a squirting
carnation or ragged wilted flower where all truth
& wisdom stems from the core stamen and casual
rapport of pillow talk, while from a zen-buddhist
perspective all just at an obscure eternal loss which
is keen lucid fluid and more than articulate & explainable

❀

i pose the philosophical question
does the husband give out before
all the appliances and if you were
to sincerely probe the wife which
one would she choose and would
any of that in the long-run matter?

❉

think i just need me one of those
nice kind waitresses in her gold
uniform pulling pencil out of bun
& taking my order coming back
with combination platter & seltzer
& lemon to last long enough to hang
out in window all day long season after season
& contemplate the madness & suffering of the world

❉

old men weeping in the park lamenting lost love

❉

the only area that dysfunctional family
deserves is the interrogation room and can
only come out til get a true-blue confession

❉

why is it that liars always seem to get
real 'defensive and offended' pissy and
hostile when you find out they're lying
as if you've somehow found out
the secrets to their character

❉

behind every joke there's always a little truth—
would that thus preclude by that mathematical
rule 'the law of opposites' a hell of alot
of bullshit to this thing called living?

☼

i stay away from specific people based on all the bs
ways they try to flatter you (which makes you feel
awfully lonesome) while prefer to spend full days
just sitting in the window of a diner looking
out at all of humanity in the lower east side
and past lives of acquaintances & strangers

☼

there is so much more in a fluttering shadow
than any of those things we address as reality

☼

what if existence and reality
is all just that unnecessary
fixating stuck inside the
boundaries of a think bubble?

☼

often the greatest faux-pas or contradiction
of thinking and reflecting is we forget about
the original instinct or set of circumstances
which led us there or within that context
(or more accurately without) may have
led us astray to completely irrelevant
places and impulsive conclusions

☼

we should try to expose our kids as much to those things
we would not ordinarily expose them to as opposed to
all those things we [so predictably] refer to as culture

❁

freedom is pedaling your bicycle madly
racing the streetcars down st. charles
avenue in new orleans as a teenager
that everpresent thick pungent aroma
of magnolia penetrating your senses
and heart & soul and finally weaving
through the french quarter of ghosts
and phantoms and madwomen to
at last plunk down on the mississippi
river and contemplate forever love and
loneliness and the spirit of your mortality

❁

loneliness kills while solitude heals . . .

❁

one should try to get used to solitary silence
like the body language and expressions of a
beautiful woman as no turning back from that

❁

yeah—all those crazy issues & drama & conflicts & crises
in this life their resolution might just be right there in front
of your eyes like just standing in front of the refrigerator
staring at some item and it being there the whole time

❁

the two-faced hypocrites always confused you
going as far back as your pre-pubescent youth

❃

tradition gradually seeing furniture get older
the same safe view of a bird's migration—

❃

if someone asked me that cliched question
"do you have any regrets?" i'd instantly answer
you asking me the question do i have any regrets

❃

"it's
not
rocket
science"
who made
that one up?
sometimes
wish it was
as would
explain
all the
reasons
i don't
wanna
get up
✺✺
✺✺

❃

on the early news two dictators
stand side by side like missiles
with ear to ear smiles for photo
ops in front of some carousel

rockets going off in the background

☼

these days seem like some psychotic badminton match
between a begrudging worn-out gigolo & old man they
throw stones at for in fact caring about his fellow man

☼

it's a weird thing in this land called amerika
how they instantly assign the local assassin
(whether successful or not) with some very
formal legal first, middle, and last name as
if giving them the significance and infamous
identity that had been eluding them for so long

☼

those petty political parasitic people
or families of dysfunction with their
clinical 'scapegoat' one feels gotta
almost commit a crime 'in order'
to prove they're alive or a nice guy

☼

has it ever been said "he's a really good guy
when you get to really not know him" as there
are so many forms of false virtue (mixed messages
and contradictions) the closer you get to people

☼

you find out who your true friends are
during periods of crisis and the advice
they give you so quixotic and bewildering
like one of those so-called sibling rivalries

✿

the quasi-virtuous or those who pretend
to be happy are the ones eventually
who will betray you in the end

✿

most aristocrats come off
as pretty damn incomplete
persnickety and petty people

✿

the best metaphor (or parable) i can think of for suburbia
was many years back living in that god awful homeowners
association while one day suddenly found myself howling
from the shadows of our garage thinking our dog had
runaway or taken off on one of his long excursions again
and remember verbalizing to myself with all this doubt and
fear this time he definitely did it then something just told
me to turn around and found him very casually staring
at me without a care in the world from the back seat of
our car as if saying what's the whole big fuss about?

✿

why does adulthood all just seem like
those afterschool futile batman episodes
where he and the boy wonder got tortured
like getting all tied up in a human knot and
could only figure out if they made it or not
by tuning in the next day touching on your
most fragile feelings and emotions wondering
what kind of life lesson were trying to teach you?

usually they got out from some silly secret trigger
or gizmo attached to their crime-fighting uniforms and
thought damn what a let down and bore this life truly was

※

when they asked the once famous comedienne
from the seventies phyllis diller known for her
crazy eccentric demeanor what she thought
about present day tv her instant reaction was
that with all the constant manic impulsive action
made her awfully nervous and anxious and often
at times could not even watch it (due to sensory
issues) while in my opinion if an alien fell down
to earth from outer space and watched tv in both the
midwest and middle east would have a very difficult
time making any distinction and not be sure which
culture and civilization was more violent or vicious

※

it's weird now seem to live in this very simplistic complicated culture
where one of the main metaphors is what if someone happens to own
a bakery and does not want to bake a cake for a gay couple or the
community happens to somehow find out their views on like homo-
sexuality or transgender (causing them eventually to shut their doors)
i mean what happened to like the year 1974 and birthday parties
and mothers dressing their kids up in nice little suits and dresses
and birthday cakes and what they referred to as party favors
i mean things in my opinion have just gotten way too serious
and maybe perhaps the baker should just be happy for them

※

i remember when very young and alone
living in that strange small city and spending
evenings just roaming the cobblestone staring
into shop windows like one showing off sharp

glistening sets of knives and cutlery another
with puppies rolling and rollicking i imagine
to try and attract and make you want to save
and adopt them (but ironically just standing there
forever down in the dumps and despondent and
feeling more a sense of abandonment) and a final
window just full of holiday mannequins dressed
up in their hats and sweaters living happily ever
after and almost felt like from a 'plato's republic'
point of view these windows in this very strange
small city was amerika's quasi view of reality

❂

catwoman stands in front
of weather map seducing
every lost male in amerika
visibility above & stocks below
had no idea how close erie was
to buffalo—our great dictator
from the hospitality field who
treats it all like some grand
monopoly board wants to
purchase in a hostile takeover
greenland the panama canal &
annex canada but your everyday
american can't even afford
the rising price of eggs
a good ole western
omelette at some
boxcar diner while
that traveling salesman
just trying to make his
quota nods-out off one
of those miniature shot
bottles by the light
of motel television

☼

last night like some lost & lonesome lone ranger
i found myself muttering man-made mantras–
"don't be so tough on yourself, you're not perfect"

☼

one can't help but to feel slight bit
situationally depressed when your
destination leads you through the
"historical district" of casinos &
cathedrals & creameries to the top
of hospital hill just to get your fill
of blood pressure meds & bottle
of wine all conveniently located
at *walmart* just to make it right

☼

linguistically break down such statements
like "sight see and save" so you go to see
such sights like the eiffel tower or pyramids
take a couple snapshots and film over your
smartphone and then take off—all seems
just a bit anticlimactic while tourists
just a bunch of fake orgasms . . .

☼

i think my wife and i are both starting
to fall in love with our housekeeper
with milky-white skin big blue eyes
and silky blonde hair as think she's
something of a scandinavian tomboy
angel. i hope my wife doesn't leave me
for the cleaning lady and have to go back
to the dating scene where they always end

up asking me if i want help cleaning up my
kitchen never noticing being a single guy
while lighting those scented candles
all women are saints in one form or
another with giggles that'll kill you

✿

the toughest part of marriage was getting a double mattress
(duvet and box spring included) which always just felt was
way too far off the ground like some lost long-gone king
on his throne while just preferred that filthy futon on the
floor in the lower east side or brooklyn (feeling so much more
comfortable in my own skin) making it your evening routine to
down an old coffee can of iced tea eventually plopping down to
flashing scenes of humphrey bogart & edward g robinson always
seeming on-the-run and with that constant chaos hustle & bustle
overlooking delancey somehow seemed like i dreamed so much
better than all that very sane safety & security i found in suburbia

✿

in the morning
just a dark room
in the middle of drizzle

'nothing'
nothing at all
more healing

✿

after all the pain & suffering all you got
left & what kicks in is gratitude & wisdom

dust turning to diamonds with sunlight
streaming through the morning window

☼

what's so petty about a petty thief anyway?
every one i ever met was pretty damn street
wise with a whole grandiose vision of life

remember that *twilight zone* episode where that guy
was wasting away in his window melting down in the heat
of the world but really freezing to death having a delusional episode

yeah all pretty much came true
where the fuck is mary tyler
moore when you need her?

☼

o! those family get-togethers with those
pathetic efforts to try and impress and
show all this bizarre charisma like know
it all extras, as just seemed like such a
waste of time while how i so much more
used to prefer the freaks and scapegoats
completely left deserted misunderstood
and underestimated—poor jimmy stewart
begging for redemption and old katharine
hepburn holed-up in her attic in connecticut
with a morphine problem and leftover echoes
of foghorns counting down her time on earth

☼

one thing i've noticed culturally in amerika
"uh-duh!" is how they no longer play that
sweeping schmaltzy ambient muzac in the
background of like supermarkets & department
stores & elevators—did they also used to that too
in airports before you took off to places like disney
world or exotic vacations with your paperback &

pina-colada with a bamboo umbrella in it planning
for your future seems to me something to be said
about that when dreams just a bit more innocent

※

the best part of american hx
the advent of rock & roll
when chubby checker
got up on his piano
& finally implored
all young girls to
"come on baby
let's do the twist"
& they finally let it all
go liberated & out of control
swinging elbows & hips &
torso out on the dance floor

※

kurt cobain
    & jim morrison
spent a majority
of their lives
i ain't kidding
living in motels
right around
the ocean
swells sweeping
through keyholes
trying to get over
hangovers from
all the hangups
of civilization
can relate to them
writing haiku to
that waitress

in west
virginia

✣

1. it is my belief that amerika lost its innocence
& never quite recovered after jfk got assassinated
& his brains blown out all over the pavement of the
parade route in dallas shown in slow-motion instant
replay over & over again 2. jackie o trying to crawl
to safety out the back of the convertible in her pink
pillbox hat camelot shattered 3. later on his brother
taken out at *the ambassador* & martin luther at that
motel in memphis 4. to the neverending quagmire
in vietnam which dragged on forever & ever never
ending 5. feeling betrayed & taken advantage of
by that crooked president richard millhouse nixon
6. desensitized by inflation & those long gas lines
7. all those americans blindfolded & taken hostage
humiliated & being paraded through the mean streets
of tehran 8. eventually the one man trying to bring peace
to the world gunned down at *the dakota* 9. remember being
a junior in highschool getting gas in my parent's oldsmobile
station wagon hearing about it over the local rock n' roll
station *wnew* in new york & tears just rolling down my
cheeks lowering my head in silence while don't recall
it getting much airplay or talked about too much in school
& just like the golden rule whole freakin fucked-up nature
& mentality of melankolia & amerika like some great big
dysfunctional family from the old country who lives by
the saying of better to be seen & not heard ie apply all
these examples & images doesn't quite seem to work

❁

has anyone ever put an old ancient vase
of heroin in their sunny kitchen windowsill
like they might do a kid's diorama or terrarium
& not follow any of those old psychological
behavioral patterns of abuse or addiction
but mostly just as needed while nodding
out to the morning early-noon paper
the world news & *standard & poors*
sports & weather tea & crumpets &
the sound of the sea & mailwoman

❁

jesus comes back for his resurrection
to the dead end with flashing christmas
decorations but gets so overwhelmed
on a sensory level develops instant
symptoms of dizziness & vertigo
wired & wasted eventually says
to himself this just ain't worth it
& nothing can save them last
scene disappearing in thin air
on some *greyhound* staring out
the window bleary-eyed, tearful
like that dynamic duo of joe buck
& ratso rizzo never quite making
it down to their destination down
to the sunshine state of florida
yet still with something of a pained
smile with the escaped boys from
the group home & cosmetologists

❀

if they didn't get jesus that day on the cross
would have just found another way to knock him off

❀

history is merely a broken record
of megalomaniacs trying to keep
up with (keep down) the masses

❀

they're all just a bunch of imitators
and if imitation is the sincerest form of flattery
where is the originator and feel so goddamn lonely

❀

we measure love by the amount of guilt we feel

❀

in this life you go through so much abuse and neglect
much later on you love when those pretty young girls
playfully make fun of you whose false accusations
become a demented form of distorted truth. . .

❀

looking back were all freaks
wrestling with our identities
leaving so much to be desired

❃

a good thing for a philosopher
is not to be believed in
in their childhood

❃

those with the need to always act stable
come across as rather foolish & insecure

❃

those who blindly don't listen
to the other side of the story
(all that gossip & rumors)
come across just as guilty
(if not more) of everything
you're being falsely accused of

❃

man believes himself to be different
and distinct in his complacency

❃

most people's promises are like false advertisements
(pithy proclamations and convenient excuses)
for all those things in their past they
didn't follow through on or failed at

❃

descartes and the great existentialists
like jean-paul sartre did not ask the right
questions when they spoke and probed
about proof of our existence as what's

more germain and accurate is people's
complacency not returning messages
which makes one feel [alienated] like they
don't exist along with their constant and
convenient vacillating of morals and
ethics to work to their own advantage

✿

the great thing about hypocrites is how they
always seem to conveniently be standing together
always for one of their self-promoting celebrations
(like clueless tourists ironically not by coincidence
literally thinking 'the world revolves around them')
pretending to be all virtuous but in fact the opposite
being more than alienating passing instant judgment
about shit they know absolutely nothing about twisting
the saying "in unity there's strength" to their advantage
but to me seems like a whole hell of alot of cowardice

✿

i think we really start to get depressed
when we find out everyone is really full
of shit full of rhetoric while feel that real
hollow sense of emptiness (of deep down
desertion and abandonment) so alone in
the universe and that one soul who actually
follows through something of a miracle like
a breath of fresh air and temporarily an end
to the blues and can hold out a little bit longer

✿

with this whole social media thing
and people's needy addictions doing
all their shit from a very safe distance
i preferred when that paper boy doing

his daily rounds on his *schwinn* bicycle
just flung the news of the world in mid
air on your front lawn while in many ways
developed far more of a 'social' human rapport

☼

when they no longer speak yiddish to you
you know you are doomed; all those cute
musical nicknames, like suddenly getting
blacklisted due to some sorta sin or shame

☼

if dreams were just half the thing
sometimes more the thing
often all the thing

if only there weren't that thing . . .

☼

as a teenager used to literally runaway
from *port authority* and take *greyhounds*
across the whole blessed bleary-eyed map
of amerika without stopping through the deep
dark neverending desert night just seeing the
snake eye lights of ghostlike trucks zooming
by ending up in cities like reno which would
just suddenly show up like lit-up oasis paradises
crossing the sierra-nevadas to san francisco simply
springing up out of nowhere from the pacific ocean
in the misty morning in awe like a miracle literally
wiping the stardust from my eyes like some
lost fugitive child trying to make a new life

✺

philosophy is turning away from bad advice

✺

the mind those blinds slightly open
casting shadows from the outside
motivating and inspiring reflection

✺

language takes on the form
and configuration of
the lay of the land

✺

satire—its beat-up broken bones
while you're just barely holding on

✺

'all this misinformation' while in that there lies
the absurd core problem (one's [in]ability to be
so easily swayed and persuaded) as opposed
to just using simple basic instincts and intuition

this all spiritually, intimately comes before
the fucked-up formulaic language of the masses

✺

they got this thing called "gig-speed"
never quite sure what that means
the thinnest iphone
scrolling . . .

with these self-important
expressions & affectations
as if doing something real
exclusive & talented

the ancient egyptians
believed in reincarnation
mummification & put up
pyramids just to prove it

like the beauty of a young
girl's simple spare knee
piercing through the
rip of a pair of jeans

worrying literally
gets you nowhere

✺

a perplexing paradoxical psychological phenomenon
how sometimes may feel more a fear of success than
a fear of failure, as when you get there feels like very
little to look back on; one can feel 'hollow' or episodes
of both acute anxiety and trepidation—a good and decent
comparison might be the psychological condition "dissociative
fugue" which can best be explained in taking a train ride and
not remembering or having any idea how you got there. . .

✺

that psychological phenomenon where
tom sawyer & huckleberry finn show up
to their own funeral—for me just wanna see
the cold cut platter and bring home a doggie bag

❈

the essence of most humor comes from
the desperate & absurd passionate need
& keen spirit to just make things better in
a world which can get awfully lonesome

❈

real true-blue diversity is who
you choose to masturbate to

❈

the benefit of the imagination
is you never have to come back
with such pithy responses like
"i wish i was making that up"

❈

be careful—you may be the best one of them all!

❈

those who attempt to act eccentric
for the most part end up at best
mediocre and adequate. . .

❈

every great artist must take the chance
in being branded a fool by the critics & masses
i mean honestly who the hell needs them anyway?

❊

i guess if life is the opposite of those stages
of mourning and can't remember a single one
of them might as well just get on with living

❊

try not to think too deeply about it
—there are a couple other senses
that'll do the trick and well worth
it and can actually be relied on
which will ironically bring you
right back to it and even do
some healing and might
possibly solve the problem

❊

once you get through all that anxiety
it's like some simmering campfire
stimulated sedated sighing feeling
closer to that thing called sanity

❊

beware that ole expression "two steps back one step ahead' '
you're not too hard-headed and too much on the edge . . .

❊

why do aristocratic women always seem
so miserable & mean-spirited (even sexually
repressed & neglected) when involved in certain
childhood pleasures like licking ice cream cones
in their poor rich girl jackie o. sunglasses at ice cream
stands in those upstanding higher-than-holy historical districts

✺

the "noble husband" (with the good reputation and
good job & good 'family man') who just naturally
cuts the lawn for the lady next door not always
so noble if you know what i'm talking of

✺

divorcees and stranded women were always the best
cuz desperate and willing to take chances and experiment
and act-out all their repressed fantasies and you were like sure
why not (got nothing better to do) as just as deserted and abandoned
and might even show up to your door with something like couple bandanas
and blindfold and some sorta gag but seemed more like a gag gift as really
not so much into it while used to follow their exact directions and tie them
to the headboard but used to joke how they ended up talking so much more

✺

with women it's all about
reading between the lines
and once you've figured them out
have already changed their minds

✺

women hate women for doing the act of seduction better

✺

women (one on one against each other)
will start wars and the pettiest of battles
while men left in the middle playing the role of
dumb diplomats trying to figure out their origins

✽

i do not have a single regret about any past relationships
i have had with women as absolutely every last single one
of them helped to heal or mend (a bit) any past trauma
or damage and for that i am eternally grateful helping me
to become a more complete, well-rounded, deeper individual

✽

any woman willing to defend you
is a woman worth fighting for

✽

those taboo women (they said were bad for you)
who took the most chances (on an intimate & intellectual
level) the ones ironically you always think about the most

✽

women love when you declare your love for them
then will try to destroy it every chance they can
drive you crazy while just gotta move on
then more times than not try to get back
in touch as if had second thoughts

✽

more women should undress
in front of their window in amerika
remember one time driving graveyard
in manhattan and suddenly this girl
like a vision just showing up at dusk
completely naked as if just getting out
of the shower getting ready for the evening
and had the most beautiful bosoms you'd
ever want to see knowing exactly what

she was doing and that simple single
seductive scene kept me returning
to that window (at that exact hour)
trying to recreate and recapture that
moment but tragically to no avail yet
trying to relive it at least got me going
and motivated (whether through fact or
fantasy) and i swear imbued my mundane
reality for the time being no longer feeling
like a complete stranger with a whole
new sense of purpose and meaning

✿

first love always seems to be about timing
(coming when you least expect it} while ironically
simultaneously finally losing a whole sense of it

as if at last you never existed and
instantly forgetting any the unnecessary
and extraneous bullshit which preceded it

✿

first love always leaves you confused
in a sort of beautiful brooding way

✿

some of our deepest and greatest curiosity
and fascination liberation and revelations
happen during that intimate and spiritual
period of first love which naturally intuitively
experience as a whole other dimension
(our senses so keen and perceptive)
and stimulating sensation of pure
transcendent bliss and happiness

❀

when you get on with marriage
often there appears to be something
of a subtle role-reversal of sensitivities
and morals and values—even romantic
proclivities due to one's time on earth & mortality

❀

the best class i took in social work school
was called "family systems" where the teacher
taught us how marriage was a constant checks
and balances which i didn't quite believe or buy
into it until a fellow student the wife of a rabbi
confirmed it and said with great conviction
that yes in fact it was definitely true and
now living the dream can say if don't
constantly check in and keep your balance
(considering moods and emotion) can totally
get out of hand even go bouncing without
the proper amount of communication . . .

❀

the other day i got
into a fight with wife
as claimed do you even
know what emojis are for?
i thought i did as sent over
a couple with upside down
smiling faces while she had
just gotten into it with a mean
spirited metermaid & was trying
to validate how it was all so fucked
up & backwards & said she was sorry
how she didn't quite get it & made sure
not to follow up with one of those *myob's*

or *lmao's* so as not to get myself into any
more unnecessary trouble & just stick with
the basic chinese & chocolate & flowers . . .

※

you try to keep them happy usually
for reasons far more deeper & shallow

※

a child's imagination and dreams
is a pebble being skimmed along
the sea leaping and flying in mid-
air and motion heading towards
no particular necessary destination

※

kinda ironic how your absent-minded kid
who gets straight a's and without a mean bone
in his body the other day just lost his watch and
metronome—you couldn't make stuff like this up

my wife has developed a relationship
first name basis with the custodians
from his school constantly having to
retrieve the homework from his locker

※

you casually mention to your son
not to put so much stock in role models

more so lounge singers
& older women

those who are around
when you really need them

❀

about the only ones
u can trust & rely on
r the garbage men & mailmen

        now can see y
            the junkies
                turned to heroin

❀

girl from the bronx
when she gets
situationally
depressed
doesn't
turn to
yoga or
gardening
but goes
through
the car
wash
got
one
of those
all you
want
wash
& dry
coupons
for a month

✼

my favorite nurses were always the smart and perverted ones
who got into it for all the wrong reasons and left you hanging

✼

i always found the secretaries
to be so much more competent
and charming than the doctors
who could use a whole hell of a
lot of training in bedside manner

✼

they never seem to ever fire those really bad people
in administration or human resources not exhibiting
a single ounce of humanity, kindness, compassion, but the
ones ironically out in the field actually doing all the hard work
and labor (having to meet their quota) won't think twice about
it matter of fact almost becomes a hardwired sociological habit

✼

why does it always seem like all those supervisors or managers
are like natural thieves (without conscious) neither representing
the paradigm of integrity or honesty cause have the leverage
and nepotism and can abuse power and get away with it

✼

for the most part the citizens are so much better
than their chosen government who just happen to know
how to [manipulate and take advantage] work and beat the system

✺

man seems to pride himself
in all the people he's got
"working under him"
as if 'making up'
a big piece of his
identity and anyone
who is willing to listen

✺

people fly flags for purposes of pride and identity
but also these days passive-aggressively (and in
a hostile manner) to try and get under your skin

✺

after the attempted assassination you fall in love
with the signer over your television who of course
does no speaking but very expressive and imagine
making love to her which in my opinion the resolution
for grownup's complete poor lack of communication

✺

almost all grownups just become fluent
in talking from both sides of their mouths
while if you happen to call them out on it
instantly get 'defensive & offended' ironically
not so much anymore eloquent when exposing their
hypocritical passive-aggressive character & behavior

✺

they only seem to love you
when they sense you're suffering

then become like some fucked-up
distorted version of love thy neighbor

※

in the end it all comes back to haunt
you even if you were a good & decent
individual and went all out for people

※

beware—those you scapegoat (or throw stones at)
may be far more psychologically and spiritually better
than all of them put together and subconsciously choose
to do so 'cause deep down inside far more innocent
substantial and loyal than can ever hope to imagine

※

in the case of family dysfunction you're guilty
until proven innocent and can take a whole life
time (to disprove) if you even care to get into it

※

"making a name for yourself—"
what an odd quirky absurd
paradoxical play of words

※

wouldn't it be nice if they paid their respects
while you were still alive? why do i need that
when i'm dead? i already know what it is i did

❀

how come i keep on remembering
& you keep on forgetting?
the strange paradox
between man
& woman

❀

you know deep down inside your wife
really loves you if gives you the leeway
and freedom to make a complete imbecile
and fool of yourself then instantly retorts by
mocking and ridiculing you in front of the kids

❀

mind over matter
what's the matter?

❀

to have to remind someone to care
or give a damn like trying to find
an answer to an unsolvable crime

❀

people are satisfied with wrong conclusions—
what absurd (delusional) simple complicated
lives and existences they all must lead . . .

❀

dreams often present as a form of spiritual neglect

☼

we often dream cause we just have the need
—to get to those core wants and needs and when
necessary the dynamic of pure escapism and fantasy

☼

besides just the subconscious i'm firmly convinced
there's a 'linguistic subconscious' (internal dynamic)
which is naturally connected to the image and form
(that is being spiritually brought up or talked about)
spontaneously (stream-of-conscious) triggering a
whole new (but very similar in substance, mood,
theme and context) language & conversation

☼

for some reason in amerika somewhere
around middle school they mandate and
force you to learn a second language (for
purposes of 'mind expansion and culture')
but with a whole hell of alot of resistance for
that self same reason of being a requirement
you know most likely in real life will probably
never use and have to learn all those grammatical
rules and memorize whole lists of outdated contrived
expressions yet if somewhere down the line happen
to eventually get the opportunity to visit that land
never really get the chance or exact context
(or 'experience') to use these very specific
vague expressions while interestingly get
more fluid or fluent when exposed to these
[strangers] natural natives or inhabitants
similar to the machinations of that toddler
or infant (with their predisposition for language)
who intuitively learns through exposure imitation
and mimicking in cadence on a lyrical musical level

✺

language is the subtle subliminal
manifestation of onomatopoeia

✺

mostly i agree with wittgenstein but what i think
he fails to mention is that people just don't listen
and thus therefore hitherto the lack of full and clear
lucid processing and comprehension of information
as well as the proper use and functioning of language

✺

beneath all that built-up scar tissue
the beating palpitating transcendent soul

✺

if only in the medicine cabinet
it read–"will prevent ghosts"

✺

pride is all we got left
when got nothing left to live for

✺

does it not seem those we try so desperately
to impress are the exact ones who
made us originally depressed?

❁

to be "brutally honest"
one wonders all the struggle
and suffering to having reached
that phase & phrase of brutal honesty

❁

on kleptomania—the act of acting-out literally reaching out for help
(sticking deep down your pocket) rebelling against authority without
even being aware of it and trying to steal back from all those people
who spiritually stole from you while simultaneously desperately trying
to connect with society for a sense of self, identity, and 'belonging'

❁

suburbia—what an absurd [unnatural] resolution to evolution
where survival of the fittest whoever's best at hiding the secret

❁

almost every great war or battle
started from something of a distorted
thought pattern somewhere between a
grandiose episode & state of severe paranoia

❁

our best grasp of culture
is just standing outside it
coming & going as you please
at your own free will & volition

❂

you develop a sense of fashion
from all those nostalgic things
left hanging in the closet
you can't quite have

❂

i wasn't sure if it was just a dream or i had just woken up from one
but suddenly viewed the whole history of the world as some cardboard
sneaker box being struck by a whole bunch of strobe lights—the whole
holy land of haifa tel aviv & jerusalem & golden dome of the rock of jews
& arabs inside—inside some weird diorama & thought man this is what
the whole damn history of civilization has come down to & best we
could do? remember being there in the late seventies & suddenly
spontaneously getting this second bar-mitzvah in my beach hat
by some very old rebbe by the wailing wall & after each & every
prayer him going "say amen" as what else could i do but to follow
his pedantic rules 'say amen, amen. . .say amen, amen. . .say amen,
amen' while like to shout out one now in the here & now present
amen for all those very poor victims on october 7th amen for
the poor starving residents of gaza amen for the people of iran
& lebanon as have had some really close friends out there in queens
& brooklyn & were some of the kindest & most sympathetic & supportive
you'd ever want to know so as that old rebbe said back there at the wailing wall
say amen amen! amen! amen! amen! to the whole cotton-pickin race of man amen!

❂

man—imagine if this president was jewish?
how they'd accuse him of being a total schyster
and cheapskate as the assassins would be lining up

❊

gotham with all its orange oompa-loompa makeup
on been taken over by the joker i swear ain't making
this up; at least with biden i guess who looks a bit like
bruce wayne's butler does care and give a damn about
his fellow man as opposed to having already declared
on his first days of office gonna take revenge along with
his fellow madmen—the penguin riddler and catwoman

❊

on those great big flashing marquees
in las vegas you got barry manilow
barbra streisand elvis impersonators
world federated wrestling and candidate
for the next president of the united states
you can try and make a distinction but is
any of that really relevant or necessary?

❊

it seems the most spiritual people
always have some sort of shtick
& scheme & charge you a fee

boy screams at his mom
in fortune-telling booth:
"you don't know what
you're speaking of!"

❊

culture is getting off
the long line at the louvre

✣

if only politics wasn't so political
(merely a microcosm of human nature)

✣

[democratic] politics has such idealistic origins
but when the dynamic of human nature gets taken
into consideration (its vulgar 'will to power and
self-interest' and willingness to betray and back
stab without conscious) "practically" the opposite

✣

politics (being both predictable & obvious
cut-throat & calculated) not only dysfunctional
& nepotism but not too far off from being incestuous

✣

imagine growing up with a narcissistic father
and munchausen mother one feels like a
stand-up comedian in an empty theater

✣

man i kinda miss those days when you'd see
like norman mailer on *the dick cavett show*
foucault going at it with noam chomsky
john & yoko janis joplin & raquel welch
who ironically had a pretty deep thoughtful
insightful opinion—nowadays you'd have
comics like woody allen & lenny bruce
getting booed off the college campus stage
for quasi-virtuous politically-correct reasons
all seems to me the rise & fall of civilization

✺

1. an invitation to the resurrection

2. donations very much appreciated

3. everything-must-go

4. laminated bibles

5. mugshot playing cards

6. dream come true finally being part of the club

7. kkk supreme court police benevolent association

8. prime rib & all the shrimp you can eat

9. rsvp not necessary . . .

✺

i don't know it's the little stuff when you live alone
or get older that really seems to matter like seeing
bagel lox and cream cheese on the menu practically
having an orgasm whether in some diner in brooklyn
the upper east side or even the caribbean. i can't stand
shit like museums or tourists but bagels lox and cream
cheese my weakness while they always seem to stack
too much on it and very strategic to order an extra plain
bagel with tin foil as know i got a bright future ahead of
me and it's the little things like this when you live alone in this
brutal existence that really seems to matter and make a difference

in my opinion we're all just leftover pavlovian pickles . . .

❃

midnight cornflakes
with tears streaming
down my face watching
the whole world go down
in flames dreaming in my
burning room seeing the
seasons change in my
window in new orleans

❃

we yearn in our dreams while even yearn
a little more (trying to recapture
that feeling) in reality

❃

we often seem to appreciate beauty most
with our whole world falling down all
around us the mist weaving in & out
of the morning mountain engulfing it
in a plume of holy glowing firmament
the simple spare sound of that wild
gurgling river with window slightly ajar
the hypnotic rhythmic placating motion
of the ocean the silhouetted skyline at dusk &
dawn a woman's naked raw body of all different
shapes & forms on top of yours with eyes closed
all coming back to haunt us in a sorta beautiful way

❃

has anyone ever been chiseled
             away at their excavation
  & just found hysterical
          doesn't necessarily
                have to be

       shakespearean
  while seems
    as good of a way
      to go as any i know
as doesn't matter
 ancient civilization
     or generation
      after generation
 a much younger
    girl's gonna
     kill you
        in one form or the other . . .

❉

whenever i'm feeling down & out & real blue
i turn to the tennis channel to watch those
pretty young women not necessarily for
their beauty but for all the other little
things like their delicate knees slim
alabaster popsicle stick legs dainty
elbows & graceful shoulder blades
blushing faces, always moving like
pigtails or braided ponytails out of
the way self-conscious with their
timid demeanor not yet at that
crucial stage with moods or
moodiness or erratic 'swings'
of behavior where they can
manipulate men & have their
way with them & drive them
crazy but thankfully still daddy's
little girl dangerous daughters
going at it with their competitor
back & forth back & forth back
& forth in a real-life literal power
struggle which proves to be cathartic

feeling totally relieved & redeemed
having absolutely nothing to do with it

✻

for every young man i recommend the romance
of what first love can do for you as opposed to any
those things having to do with morals ethics or principles

✻

i used to love those black & white videos
of like those surreal silent home movies
of jim morrison & the doors sitting back
in cushy limo on the way to the concert
peaceful, thoughtful, brooding, and soon
would be goaded on by that mob mentality
and would become something between
self-destructive and his own personal
crucifixion; truth not always a good
thing—so says lenny bruce, socrates

✻

we must also put a little time
aside to watch the snow flying
in the morning listening to all
of schubert's masterpieces—

abbott & costello meet the mummy . . .

✻

the impeccable comedians get you too
with their body language and expressions
and timing and pacing—there's not a whole
hell of alot of dramatic actors can say that about

❋

almost every great actor
happened to have a huge heart
and would bare it all and fall apart
for that [apathetic] audience "in the dark"

❋

did the fiddler on the roof
ever just have a really bad
night & refuse to come down
& holler & howl vulgarities
in yiddish & just climb up
a bit further to overlook
the whole damn shtetl
& universe having revelations
& after being totally drained
& his wild tangle of beard
drenched in rain returns
back to his wife's bed
a little more sane
knowing deep down
inside always be welcome

❋

we are all hurt & damaged actors
and spend the rest of our lives
trying to recapture that starring
role which seemed lost so long ago

❋

yer final scene
may it all be
like one of those
bergman dreams

or was it fellini
all empty & bleak
cobblestone by the sea
gruenbaum's bakery
fellow delinquent
comedian thieves
those wild turkey
roaming to *the*
shakespeare
festival
somewhere
between
the dusk
& evening

✿

dreaming—opening your eyes to reality
and trying to close them again
to denying and surviving

✿

nightmares—like trying to get all this shit out your system
being brought up on charges by all these mistaken identities

✿

symbolism—what's leftover from all suffering (not having
the experience or knowledge or able to relate) reading too deeply

✿

superstition—a distorted thought pattern/overcompensation
panacea to those things acutely anxiety-provoking and last-ditch
symbolic, magical, desperate effort to try and get spiritual and cognitive
control to provide a sobering sense of self, stability, sanity and self-preservation

❅

faith—all those things just out of reach
struggling (seeking) somewhere
between fact & fantasy

❅

our good long-term memories are so surreal
with a dream-like quality as if happened
a whole other lifetime ago . . .

❅

all those things that we hide and deny
and compartmentalize are the things
that mean the most to us and just
have a difficult time emotionally
expressing and making sense of

❅

my wife's dad used to cheat on her mom
alot and was never around and said
her best memories & moments
was when she saw stubble
in the sink cuz knew
he was home . . .

❅

family dysfunction
the normalizing of
abnormal psychology

❄

most of those expressions of hyperbole
are completely lacking in meaning
("i was in horror. . .i'm at a loss. . .")
and simply makes one feel guilty
and so far from reality more than likely
the path leading to self-fulfilling prophecy

it takes so long to realize (if ever)
their characterological patterns and insecurities

❄

words and definitions only
hold any true meaning once a
feeling and emotion (more times
than not a crisis) is attached to it

❄

missing-in-action only a fraction
of the equation or the remainder
(prodromal phase and symptoms)
of a condition far larger that can only
really be pictured or imagined with a
parallel conflict or crisis (image) triggers
the core state of mind you find yourself in

❄

paranoia is when the patience of a saint
runs thin and just got nothing left to offer or give

❃

all those things that we block are for reasons
far greater than we lock up in the first place

❃

one should never underestimate
their natural instinct and judgment
as natural and instinctive to finally
figure it all out and make sense

❃

all those days we thought we had it made
maybe we did and simply just did not
take ourselves seriously enough

❃

those who feel constantly judged
somewhere down the road inevitably
become a victim to their own judgment

❃

those who are not nice to each other
one can actually make the argument
are of 'unconscionable' behavior

❃

beware of those who declare their love too early
as may very well prove to be too needy and some
where down the line "control freaks" blaming and
making you the one responsible for dashing their dreams

❊

it's those simple subtle statements which are so blatant
when trying to deal with those people of clinical narcissism

❊

in the grownup world it's whoever plays with words
(a rather predictable and absurd dynamic) the best
and gives 'the impression' with their very sophisticated
casual cocktail party banter and if you should happen
to approach them for purposes of clarification get
awfully 'defensive and offended;' most successful
of this species pretend as if nothing happened and
continue with their unconvincing role play and act

❊

you find most humans are like used car salesmen
real nice and charming when they want to sell you
something—after that they never get back to you or
return messages; you wonder how they treat their women?

❊

all that false advertising they try to sell you—
no wonder as a kid a thief reaching out for help
is that one of those oxymorons or onomatopeias?

❊

politics in amerika these days are like those
two-faced mean-spirited kids who used to
talk behind your back in school; even back
then i knew they were just a bunch of fools

☼

for all those so-called contractors & editors
& past acquaintances who simply just vanished
& fell off the face of the earth i hope when their time
comes are left exactly where they were in mind body
spirit & soul—i could never be like that & remember
those insane wild summers sitting back on the steps of
the *ny public library* & how childhood flowers smelled
exactly like the perfume counter at herald square *macy's*

☼

i've always put far more trust
in those who go all out with satire
as opposed to the compulsive liars
who pretend to be sincere and honest

☼

people spend their whole entire lives trying to find
some kind of hardwired tradition even if it kills them

☼

imagine that—spending a whole life trying to prove your 'innocence'
that describes the existence of the artist [falsely accused
and unfairly convicted] becomes his conviction

☼

almost every great philosopher
at the end of their life finds themself
in some kind of literal or proverbial prison
having to defend themself against the ruthless
derision of the masses and critics—that's what
they get for speaking their mind while church

and state and politician and aristocrat found
mingling at the very exclusive barn dance

❁

wouldn't it be great if we became more valuable
like those baseball cards we collected at 8 years
old—thurman munson, pete rose, manny mota

❁

people from experiencing constant crisis
and trauma (emotional and psychological
abuse and spiritual neglect) in their very early
lives will act-out and even develop personality
disorders and whole new identities as coping
mechanisms to protect themselves and
function from all the unnecessary unjust
and overwhelming pain and suffering

❁

if we're so busy just trying to function & survive
& fail to remember any those good sentimental
times believe we're doing ourselves a grave
disservice even feels like a bit of a crime

❁

not by coincidence often those who are
the most profoundly alienated & ostracized
(can't afford to take it all for granted) prove
to be the most keenly observant & perceptive
as suffering has taught them all they'd care
to know about [the patterns of] human nature

☼

you keep on fighting your way out the corner
and i guess somehow eventually find your way
out but not so much sure how much i necessarily
agree with that old cliched proverb of what doesn't
kill you makes you stronger while maybe more
so a bit more determined defensive and guarded

☼

we learn so much more about ourselves when
we are dreaming than anything in our waking reality

☼

that very strange odd phenomenon
of faraway silhouetted skylines while
you get struck with such fear and anxiety
and apathy and trepidation when going
bumpadabumpa through the toll booths
towards that ridiculous illusory kingdom

you turn on the weather . . .

☼

bumpadabumpa hell on earth
is man's lost distorted view
of one day reaching the
pearly gates of heaven

that roll of tokens
gets him there quicker

☼

the absurd behavioral pattern of
constant routine & ritual even going
so far (without being aware of it) of
self-deprivation, while if you're always
just trying to please then when realistically
are you ever happy cause when the time comes
may very well forget the feeling of that emotion

☼

all that obsessive need for necessary perfectionism
not simply 'chemical' but a substitution and distorted
thought pattern (guilt and conflict and overcompensation
from some past spiritual loss or damage) and sense of
incompletion (still with psychodynamic need to please
and get approval however accurate or realistic is that
selfsame expectation) and profound need and desire
for recognition even [the sublimation] of redemption

☼

what happens when you have self-destructive tendencies
hardwired from past damage? the best you can do is creep
back to the original baseline where all the dreams started

☼

the best chinese i ever had
was when wife picked it up
on that strange hoity-toity
stripmall surrounded by
soulless cawkasians enough
to make you hate the 'act'
of living & casually went
in being a girl from the bronx
& picked it up & never paid

for it & went erica no you
didn't & she said well they
didn't ask & not ashamed
to admit probably the
best chinese i ever had

☼

i'd believe in the whole prison system
(incarceration & rehabilitation) if on
the last day of the sentence show just
a bit of contrition like some pathetic
corny picture of the smiling warden
& convict together even if it's
as fake & phony as one of those
phony-baloney dysfunctional families
passive-aggressively posing in the suburbs

☼

nowadays you got the stretch limo
for both the dictator & assassin
that spoiled obnoxious family
getting picked up at their mcmansion

☼

the conflict & confusion of contexts
is what has confounded the philosophers
over the ages—their removal an instant answer

☼

man has a tendency at his very own convenience
to take 'practically' everything out of context.
it is the rare few & intelligent upon reflection
who have the ability to do the opposite—

❊

we gather our truths from all those false hoods
& lies like the best wine coming from rocky soil

❊

has an excavation ever been done
merely for reasons metaphysical
and that ancient eternal spirit
feeling and knowing it exists
digging deeper just to prove it?

❊

if only the church people had the character & behavior
of those people they so boldly pompously represented

at best they're those friends from junior
high school who promised to get back to you

❊

generosity is natural & inherent
while doesn't just come at one's
own convenience & self-interest

❊

with the jealous & envious
due to the nature of their
character & behavior
never know you're
at war with them

✽

all that cliched bullshit and nonsense
about making a good first impression
when ironically more times than not
wasted on those gaslighting not
particularly well-intended and
passing instant judgment
fallen angels fly south for the winter

✽

in a cliched way they say
don't burn your bridges
why not? some clearly
need to be burned
to gain a whole
new perspective

✽

all these reenactments of jesus christ
               if we had only done it right the first time
dear charles atlas,
      & stick dollar in envelope
running back & forth to mailbox
             getting no response
experiencing that first feeling of betrayal
                 & all-out hollow emptiness & loss

✽

even when you try to act like a saint
they treat you like a criminal—

no self-pity here
just hell of lotta
proclamations

made up of
half-truths

the martyrs are
unconvincing actors

❁

what happened to the comedians?
the classic rock n' rollers?
yul brunner puffing
his cuban . . .

❁

does it not seem like most of them
in that audience (of 'culture') are just
clapping for themselves (in a certain
form of self-adoration) self-absorbed
on a pseudo-intellectual level, while
in my opinion most forms of gratitude
and appreciation would just be pure
zen-buddhist silence, as the spiritual
artist ('of karma') knows this as well

❁

sometimes life just feels like
constantly being on trial by all
the idiots buffoons and imbeciles
who haven't paid their dues and
lived it; tragedy is denouements
turned inside-out—why you spent
so much of this existence traveling

❊

death is when the whole absurd performance
and politics of living is over. at least you got
around the world a couple times over and a
decent taste & flavor of the drama of women

babe ruth never got a call back from the yankees
which in my opinion seems something of a sin . . .

❊

at the end of our lives we get to really know
ourselves like a blind date who never shows up

❊

it was good growing up not to be taken
terribly seriously like some idiot buffoon
who couldn't stay out of trouble a cabana
boy with eyes and ears constantly open
getting secret stock tips from those
aloof & arrogant all-knowing assholes
wisdom working retail at everything
must go old money resurrection . . .

❊

all those who make such bold statements like
"looking back i have absolutely no regrets"
most likely have a ton of them due to the
fact in having to make such statements

✤

death is the final punchline to the riddle
all those people who never knew you
lining up for the cold cut platter

the rabbi & gynecologist . . .

33

if we constantly find ourselves returning to trauma
(& crisis) hardwired in the psychodynamic vicious
abuse cycle might we also parrot similar-like behavior
when desperately trying to gain recognition in the
absurd illusory hierarchy of culture & civilization?

34

be careful & cautious (even being a bit ambitious)
with the constant obsessive need to move forward
to never forget (or neglect) those precious sentimental
memories & moments where most likely all these dreams
& fantasies & spirit(s) originally got their start & existed

35

at least with noir way back when had a certain sense
of style & class; how they'd suddenly whip out their
handy cigarette or gun or naturally start powdering
their nose when feeling a pang of existential angst
when that phone unexpectedly rang in a room full
of party guests or exclusive residents you instantly knew
who did it while think there's something to be said about that

36

the only reason i never considered suicide
were all those little people leftover i thought
just not quite right for the part (in exploring
explaining & extrapolating on this life) while
just don't think i could ever live with myself

37

the ones we find totally obsessed with style
(who can't live without it) in form & function
ironically are the ones of the least substance

38

has man ever had the character to pass a nice & kind rumor?
almost every war started by a coward around the water cooler

39

you knew the suburbs were not for you
when after working long grueling days
forced & man/dated to go to these home
owner's association meetings of a lot of
petty griping where the living rooms were
separated, culturally sub/divided by genders
making it all that much more boring & obvious
(seemed like a hostage crisis on noah's ark)
like those socials you used to go to in elementary
school & so much more would have preferred to talk to . . .

40

range of human emotions
of feelings (or repressing)
of defense-mechanisms
(offensive & insulting)

the couple that kills together . . .

41

went on a cruise to save the relationship
& from everything i heard due to drinking
& womanizing not even an sos could do the
trick pretty much shipwrecked & sunk it &
if looks could kill in that final picture sick

42

stuff like after school on fridays
going swimming at that girl's pool
& with her girlfriend sharing blunts
& then all of us lying in her bed listening
to the grateful dead & the one in the middle
giving a massage to the one on each end i guess
being seductive & stimulating & going no further

from what i heard both of them became doctors . . .

43

we all need to be saved
like those hebrew slaves

i ruled that out quite a while ago

as wait outside one of those coffee machines
automatically making and mixing my coffee
while simultaneously, strangely, seductively

stimulated hearing that very pretty driven girl
urinating through the door of the bathroom
at *the new school for social research*

i never ever really wanted to be anybody . . .

44

when we first started dating
meeting at the *wurzweiler school
of social work* at yeshiva she bought
me these classical masterpieces and
although i didn't know a heck of alot
about classical learned to slow dance
with her in dark railroad apartment
looking over that part of cloisters
that big brightly-lit building across
the way where every so often they'd leave
their windows open and if that's not exhibitionism
getting rid of all inhibitions i don't know what is?

45

planted in bellman's closet
during my graveyard with
ezra pound's "cantos" and
burroughs' "exploding ticket"
fresh pitcher of iced tea
made by nice & classy
alcoholic bartender
& nightly slice of swiped
key lime pie from giant

refrigerator dozing-off
while farm-o-pseudo
call salesmen from
the midwest good
family men with
secret identities
return from late-night
meat market full of
drag queens ironically
nodding-out on heroin

when the sun begins rising you'll pick
the stacks of newspapers off the curb
with the passed-out drivers from hot
ice trucks & start to polish the brass
from the luggage carriers putting up
letters for cosmetologist convention

give a hearty welcome to the
puerto rican housekeepers . . .

46

one day with my wife doing all this spraying
around the house i'm gonna go down like
gregor samsa coiled in the corner while
my girl from the bronx barking "stop
overreacting!" as she takes off with
a bottle of *febreeze* in each palm

47

man sacrifices for his woman due to a strange
sort of idealized & archetypal worship for both
the image & vision; a deeply-embedded guilt,
emptiness of existence, what he thinks love is

—a mother, sister & daughter who 'get' him,
an unquenchable, penetrating spirit of being
& consciousness & a girl he's always been
head over heels in love with from the very
beginning, who will not only titillate but
also support, nurture & take care of him

48

marriage is the effort to recapture
(restore that 'innocence lost')
& secure all those things that
got taken (so impulsively)
against one's own will &
volition when not looking

49

the perfect marriage, miscarriage of justice
as claim it's all about compromise, compassion
& 'conviction' while if you didn't get her around
the world did you at least get her halfway between
galveston & gloucester where that very svelte red
& white lighthouse resembles the portrait of that
gorgeous monet blushing lady in her ivory-white
hoop dress strolling introspective contented
along the lovely lush lawns on the ocean

50

nodding-out from exhaustion in the back of a taxi
in spain the cab driver suddenly exclaims to my
wife & i "do you like the supertramp?" as from
what i heard they're usually like 20, 30 years
behind while gotta go all the way back to my

childhood & respond with giving him a little
white lie like 'yeah, they're really talented'
& goes into deep depth & detail how he
actually pulled his kids from school just
to follow them all through europe & must
admit how i really did dig his sincerity &
conviction as well as intellectual curiosity
which honestly always felt in my rapport &
exchange with certain people like parisienne,
spanish, greek cab drivers so much more than
most americans i had ever been in contact with
as we raced through the orange orchards & pecan
trees of andalucia & finally got dropped off in the
jewish quarter safe & sound in the shadows of sevilla
as to me in my opinion what real culture was all about

Cure for Insomnia

i have always loved spain
most especially madrid
where the old men
in their long matador
moustaches are planted
over long flowerbeds
of red & white geraniums
watching those young
pretty girls with tiny
champagne cup
bosoms & long
popsicle stick
legs & rosy cheeks
competing against
each other on the
red clay tennis courts
i've never been very much
a big fan of the aristocrat

but in this case dig the
old men in their matador
moustaches very serious
popping up from behind
the flowerboxes of
red & white geraniums
watching these gorgeous
killers go against each other
these old money old timers
with their matador moustaches
just budding from flowerboxes
of red & white geraniums entranced
with these to die for daughters
who i'd take home to meet
my mother & hopefully
never be seen from again
whether in belarus russia
morocco paris or madrid

51

0

Pray/lewd

all they keep hidden from you
turning a saint into an
instant criminal

all that wisdom which flows
from the glowing eyes
of a jack-o-lantern

all those prayers on the perimeter
of the illusory blessed cursed forest
lost somewhere between fate & reality

on the donation
of your broken holy
heart after lovemaking

on the donation
of your soul after they
steal everything from you

on the empty escape
alley way in the back
of your cluttered mind

on the cage they keep
you in to maintain both
illusion & reputation

on the weather
inside & outside
of the snowglobe

on the life & times
of the deaf dumb & blind
curator at the wax museum

An Abstract/Case Study:

you seem to only really be in touch with your true profound feelings
when catastrophically losing something taking that air-conditioned
rattling local during the sweltering summer welling-up somewhere
between the suburbs and projects to the madness of the great
metropolis experiencing the phenomenon where it all strangely
enough appears familiar yet simultaneously distant (disassociated)
all that trauma and damage must imagine the core nature of surrealism

I.

On the Nature of Surrealism

girl gives birth
to a beautiful
back alley

to the leftovers
of a fluff & peanut butter sandwich
in a wild elementary cafeteria cemetery

manifest destiny
was standing in a deep shag rug
overlooking all the mad beauty of recess

dixie cup filled up
with stars from
the night before

in the morning
in the leftover
light of the moon

getting your
baseball cards ready
for your day in school

perfectly packed
in front pockets
of canvas pants

choppy boat
sits on the
placid shore

the wild bulls sniffing all around
misty morning windows
of the castle

the palace falls down in the rainstorm
the mountain goes down over the moon
at the end of the lagoon blue skyline on fire

at the blinking tv tower a hostage crisis
which works by the opposite dynamic
implying can pretty much have him

while keeps them enamored
with versions of roy orbison
frankie lymon & the teenagers

the gorgeous impoverished
young farm girl in flannel
selling roadside pumpkins

a boy mutely sobs
still in his football
uniform in garage

true love
is sky-blue snow
on the roof of a barn

walkie-talkies found
after all the snow
melts from ground

boy just naturally
picks them up–
"o there they are"

pals play cards
all day in the
laundromat

by the sound of
the swollen river
& throbbing trains

suicidal secretaries
insanely screaming
in the wild waves

behind the dairy cream
saved by courageous teens
who wouldn't think twice

the tollbooth men
just need time away
from their wives

those lush green hills
behind the big blue
town pool where

aloof lifeguard in her
sunglasses & legs
crossed sits like

a queen up on her throne
as if saying don't bother
me—leave me alone

pretty young single
mothers with their
toddlers hanging

out in the back
of the traintracks
with a perfect view

of the aftermath
of that radiant river
rushing into mountains

the gravediggers
lean their shovels
right up against

the outside of gas station
& in the early morning
take their cup of joe

silent solemn
somber & full of soul
before entering the fields

& connecting
the mortals with
the afterworld

the airport motel lounge
all filled up with fallen angels
gods of st. cloud looking down on them

fugitives on-the-run
from the reservation
surviving g off whiskey

& corndogs
just trying
to make it

so it's true—really all just a matter
of getting it all off your chest (even if
can't reach a resolution pretty cathartic)

why probably had all those
brilliant mythological greek gods
going at it & fighting the elements

all that evil—who's that? atlas kneeling
with the whole wide world on his shoulders
in front of health club on central avenue in yonkers

an old man rides on the *greyhound* bus
with a little blue velvet box on his lap
through the dusty towns of america

humble inward minding his business
as if everything depends on this
& in many ways it does

& wish there were
just a couple more
around like him

those boys i grew up with
i guess still so fucked-up
& damaged with a sense

of desertion & abandonment
when they became husbands
found weeping in windows

when wives returning home
from law symposiums &
cosmetologist conventions

senoritas hanging
from scarlet curtains
over *south brooklyn casket*

mafioso sitting
at cafe tables chatting
keeping it all in perfect order

newspaper boy
used to roll up
your home

& toss it on
the lawn
saving

your soul
the sports
& weather

peeing beneath stars
from back door
of basement

seems so much quieter
out there in the tree
frogs after the storm

sobbing
through
keyhole

in the morning you feel
those cool pumpkin pine
floors which in fact open

up the mind heart & soul
those wild wicked winds
which have penetrated

& seeped in
somewhere
between

the subconscious
& imagination
something

to never
ever take
for granted

in the beginning of our marriage
me & my wife in the middle
of the night had to climb

out miniature windows
of that madwoman's
bed & breakfast

who wouldn't let
us leave early
who would

serve supper
at like 9:30
& everything

seemed to revolve
around her feeling
something like these

escaped fugitives
in that village
over the

clattering kitchen
of this pub & grub
but ironically feeling

more content
less worried
safe & secure

boy looks out
from group home
windows of his castle

the secret life of crossing guards
& tutors who still live with moms
like those tiny leftover crab apples

naturally fallen from branches
& down the gutters imbuing
the whole village with

the fermented aroma
of childhood wine
young handsome

sailor charms
daughter inside
cobblestone alley

the young ex-con
who gets taken care of
by a much older woman

(vice-versa) & stepchildren
on a brokedown farm on
dark side of mountain

the cute befreckled
down-to-earth tomboy
who can keep up with

any of the boys
on the dead end
which means

catching frogs
all day in the
shadows & wind

those summers as a kid
making tapes of neil young
'harvest, after the gold rush'

from warped vinyl to mint cassette
magic marker smudged diligently
writing down each & every song

just simply laying back
hanging out under the sun
wasted not quite as much

could anything
anything—nothing
at all been much better

your uncle from oceanside
tumbling in dryer to try
& win friends' favor

in a whole miniature house
wrapped in plastic furniture
half-crazed, haunted dolls

waxed fruit & grandfather
clock which counted
down your mortality

& tick-tock
time on earth
by the hour

wilted flowers in a vase
like exhausted shipwreck
survivors bent over on a

tumultuous sea—kids writing
in the top right of their paper
"today will be sunny, 1970"

bible club meeting
where they keep
the washer machines

down in
the basement
the only place

you feel safe
& secure &
stimulated

where you read
your albert camus
& jean-paul sartre

may even
get liberated
redemption

with a box
of *tide* & nice
roll of quarters

pleasantly molested
in burnt down disco
by the melancholic

seductive older sisters
with dream & desire
of finally getting

eternal approval
due to spiritual
neglect from

manipulative
munchausen elders
taking advantage

the best thing about growing up
was driving through purple shutters
to pick up chinese take-out at dusk

get so sick of these editors
playing the same boring
obvious hard-to-get roles

putting all your pain
& suffering down on paper
no royalties royalty with no soul

miss those days at yeshiva
when those ultra-orthodox
girls came on to you . . .

little boy blue
still on moon
misinterpreted

by those foolish
alcoholic firemen
going through motions

just shooting out
their ladders
arguing

about reality
& the right
expressions

on the way
to the fire
never once

ever really
considering
starry options

in being
a romantic
& the imagination

has a corner ever been busted
for hanging out too much on
the corner whistling at all

the pretty girls "send me to the corner
i been very bad!" them secretly loving
it while being hit on by all these bad

boys passed down
from generation
to generation

remember how they said
you could die if you swallowed
a whole pack of *pop rocks* with *coca-cola*

you & your pals during your child
hood hanging out in the parking lot
on the corner of the 7-11 with mouths

wide open like idiot
wiseass hippos filled
with mad scientist potions

as a teenager
with your blue
bandana on

hanging out
with pals
smoking

blunts by
the river
where

the trains
come in
in autumn

when you'd get
back home to do all that
homework felt like never

all that resistance & rebellion
nihilism touching on
your mortality

knowing every statistic
on the back of every
yankee baseball card

the stray scent of that
thin stick of bubblegum
mud & flowers & rivers

rushing
through
pachysandra

able to recollect
the dewy onion grass
scent from fields of childhood

ain't bragging at all
but was a soccer star
& used to fall asleep

like some dummy-ventriloquist
all hopeful with an idiot smile
dreaming of your future

those muddy cleats
which never got touched
in the vestibule & safe

you got for hanukkah
with a sandwich bag
full of bb's love letters

from third cousin
out in california &
couple coins from

that field trip
on a bus
out to

philadelphia
which made you
feel all 'safe & secure'

on my wall taped posters
of bob mcadoo spencer
haywood walt clyde

frazier & the rest
of the new york
knickerbockers

a little later on
ripped-out glossy
pictures of brooke shields

cheryl tiegs that
see-through netted
one piece on the beach

probably be able
to figure out my stages
of human growth & development

boyhood body
turned wrinkly
from chlorine

bloodshot eyes
& chattering teeth
reading whole stat

column for
bronx bombers
during summer

the only thing that keeps
you going these days
spring training

yanks
verse
dodgers

mildewed medicine
ball & corruption
of kulture

emaciated blue bison
the projects of las vegas
how to survive off boloney

& cheese sandwiches
kool-aid without sugar
we were so poor ate

hamburger helper
without the burger
"ha! ha! i hear ya!"

taking off from motel at the end of
the burlington northern in the early
morning already near 70 in reno

wandering like some moses-fugitive
through the desert to some ridiculous
human resources where they interrogate

you for identification having no idea
your perseverance & discipline
willingness just for a position

to work the casinos for all those loud soulless
tourist businessmen & college students
all pretty much the same all pretty

in sane how they never get back to you
& choose rather to spend your days
just as content reflecting in a state

of redemption in truckee river
contemplating the nature
of man & the universe

all those broken flowers
& promises on the billboards
looking down on you from the hills

we are all just broken jigsaw
puzzles merely searching
for the missing pieces

brooding standup comedian
taking the bus at dusk
to the nightclub

escalators just beginning to
light up purple at the movie
theater in the early evening

the hazelnuts & pecans
falling from the autumnal
trees of the drizzly city park

steam baths & pharmacist
begin to close
up shop

the telephone wires
fill up with wild
colorful parrots

always wanted to own
a very thin bookshop
in the poor part of paris

where every morning
pick a wino up off the curb
teaching me remedial parisienne

call me crazy
but spent my days in paris
surviving off brie & baguette

& take-out vietnamese
& *kronenbourg* beer
perfectly content

writing my aphorisms
in a tiny flat in montmartre
with all the shutters left wide open

fact that jim morrison decided
to stay in paris after he died
best career move in his life

colorful bullfighting posters
torn outside the coliseum
everything seems vacant

is this valencia?
you & wife take
bus back through

mountains
to that tiny
town gandia

on these hot humid
mornings i think back
to our days in andalucia

carelessly strolling through
those lush verdant courtyards
in sevilla for our breakfast of

warm goat's milk & cereal
creampuffs & champagne
those old ladies sneering

staring my wife down
i guess for innocently
wearing belly shirt

a pretty bronx girl
like some escaped orphan
partaking in spanish buffet

in my velvet castle
i want to fall asleep
by the roaring fire

a leather-bound
book by my side
while the butler

quietly tippy-toes
in & out—a do not
disturb sign wrapped

around his body
feeding logs
to the fire

to keep my
dream
alive

shutters opened
in the morning
by my bride

on the nature of the jesus christ
lizard who nimbly walks on water
on the muddy rivers of costa rica

when yer down & out
all's you need a hut
& little banana tree

right outside black sand beach window
comics & the brilliant bio "saint genet"
by the great philosopher jean-paul sartre

torrents of driving rain coming down
in the middle of the night like you're
in some sort of murderous film noir

like one of those triggers
where you just forget it all
most importantly who you are

how to write haiku
in the park in the
lower east side

at twilight
nursing quart
of *ballantine*

when the empty
pool on pitt street
fills up with fall leaves

spending whole days
surviving off 50 cent
frankfurters on 6th

avenue in
the west
village

holes in
the souls of
tennis sneakers

literally feeling
the soft melting
pavement beneath

your feet drag queen
kicking the shit out
of macho man

sick of being
made fun
of by him

who discovered
the city of
manhattan?

pioneer hotel
on the border of
little italy & chinatown

those ole time
black & white
smokestacks

of ships like
the top hats
of infamous

industrialists
politicians
pickpockets

thieves
& slapstick
comedians

silent chinese gang
just sits in blinking belly
of firefly flashing evening

those fireflies flashing
past your window like
the broken blinking bulbs

of ole mafia photographers
whipping out their cameras
snapping pictures of your beat

brokedown brooding
body just trying to
make things right

the gigantic glow-in-the-dark
cross up in the hills overlooking
alcoholics anonymous & used car lots

a whole lost broken down town
just filled up with runaways & vagabonds
who only come out at night to hustle the shore

like those carnival workers
& silent movie stars used to get
picked up for disorderly conduct

hygienists
claw each
other in ditch

the summer
actors the only
ones who exist

ice skating rink
hidden deep in a
dense patch of trees

right where
the cape
begins

& have those
rows of cottages
planted on ocean

lobster rolls
& lost souls
with all those

downlow family
secrets & opiate
& drinking problems

pictures in picture
frames you're not
supposed to talk of

at funerals you can
always sense the loss
with their cats & dogs

the amphibians
on the side
walk . . .

two blue nuns stroll
past a proud old broken
man in his wrinkled linen

suit & fedora who sits
on a park bench beneath
the palms of paradise while

with fate such a sacred fine
line between sin & sacrifice.
in this part of town where

they keep all the madmen
& diners a perfect place to
lose yourself & reminisce life

woolworths
winnemucca
wannamakers

all necessary places
for man to lose himself
in the history of amerika

he drove one of those caged vehicles
at the driving range where all those
horrible very driven businessmen

took aim at him
like some human
pinata being flogged

by soulless mannequins
was this one of those jobs
where all those privileged

know-it-all assholes
who've never had
to work a day

in their lives
refer to as an
honest living?

the history of culture & civilization
a demented form of exhibitionism
right before & after the stoning

struck with insomnia ain't sure if it's
the televangelists filling up the stadium
or just those spirited geriatrics in *the mall*

of america with their token plastic spine
& skeleton & surgeon in his white coat
& stethoscope or simply might be that

madman phil swift with his miracle
adhesive made to stop up all those
holes in your soul, gutters & keep

you afloat while for some strange
reason in amerika to always prove
it have some massive steam roller

running over the product to show
how it instantly pops right back
into shape & is unbreakable

how your reality & being
will be if purchase in the next
15 minutes & fall right back asleep

after a night full of goddamn
freakin' nightmares you wake
up to some gigantic wild turkey

suffering struggling to get up
your hill like some old yenta
carrying a bag of kosher goods

& think damn maybe you just don't
have it all that bad while turn to a life
of reading daily obituaries & perhaps

making black currant jam—pear
tarts & apple pie from the orchard
you've been working on for so long

weird weather
makes for wild
strange insane gardens

the holy huff & puff
of the radiator
beneath red mountain

just down the road
an old-fashioned
general store

with creaky warped
wooden floors, a paper,
sliced cheddar, cold cuts

& some sweet kind
red headed owner
just to make small

talk with to make
sure you're all's
ok in the world

all those new england homes
screened-in wraparound porches
surrounding the town ball field

kids returning back
to vestibules after a
twinight doubleheader

listening to blues
with summer lover
some time after

midnight in
revolutionary
war graveyard

woodpecker bangs
its bill against the
side of the barn

as a form
of mating call
doesn't sound

all that bad
as we're all
so desperate

& out of control
ventriloquist with
leftover uniform

fortune in a heap
of crumbs & squirting
carnation tells you your future

u stick your head out
the holy impoverished
summer window taking

in the mist from the mountains
like some ship going down finally
smelling the roses & chinatown alleys

finding myself unable to get up this morning
just sitting on the edge of my bed suddenly
out of nowhere chant "six foot two, eyes

are blue, richie cohen is after you, six foot
two, eyes are blue, richie cohen is after you"
this kid who way back in the day in summer

camp, like some sort of mythological god
would hit monster homers & literally had
to just stop the other game in the outfield

to watch, as would drift all the way out there
wondering where richie cohen is right now
think was a kid from jersey or the island

(there is a sleepwalker convention
& psycho-farm-logical symposium
at one of those modern lavish hotels

which looks like some svelte
shimmering castle rising from
an ancient field of rice paddies

wild wolves wailing
in the decadent lobby
of very old money who

died behind their papers
some time ago that very
driven businesswoman

with her token complaint
of bedbugs & the young
hotel clerk required to make

the exchange when she
isn't there rummaging
through panty drawer

& takes a souvenir
to get him through
his swing shift

the sound of secretaries
clomping past the window
at dusk or could be one of

those police horses while none
of it really matters just trying
to get through this reality

like the old retired
merchant marine
shrunken night

watchman just standing
at the front door of
the hotel & when

the sun goes down
each & every evening
like some insane tradition

for no apparent reason
just howling due
to hallucinations

or as if literally
seeing his whole life
pass right in front of him)

guess the best time to become a drunk
in your later life in the early dusk
chilling & warming up

the wrong wines
to help you
get by

like jesus h. christ's
last supper in front of
the local sports & weather

superman
eating tv dinner
in shattered glass slipper

(somewhere between
suicidal & giving
up the business

having revelation
that triggers are just
simply fragile demeanor

histrionic, haunted
of being afraid of
one's own shadow

& the only thing
that can possibly save us
is the 'desensitization' of

that sudden strange
self-destructive
& selfsame

image
feeling
& emotion)

crank on the old
smashing pumpkins
as tuna fish on matzoh

will get you
through the
crisis of living

all's i need some
ole time frauline
to take care of me

apple pie
& ice cream
& drizzling expected

do not disturb sign
to keep away the
envious & jealous

wonder what topeka
the beaches in texas
really like leave it all

to my girl from the bronx
cuz a good sport
& really knows

what it's like
to suffer &
try so hard

puerto rican girls rub
garlic on their fingernails
to scratch each others eyes out

blackboy puts raw
chicken in crate
& tosses over

pier to attract crab
& cook up with beer
& pepper & *shake & bake*

pit bulls bark
from the rooftop
to keep eye out on cops

the exact same
bloodshed on the
exact same corner

in the early morning
right after the dawn
at the bottom of

the subway steps
in coney island where
the rickety rollercoaster

& fried chicken joints
are draining their neon
the one-armed cook flips

hashbrowns with a spatula
for the cops & robbers simply
minding their own reading the paper

all those ex-cons
sleeping with one
eye open on the train

to the last stop in brooklyn
hold the secret truths &
mysteries of the universe

all i remember was that broken
down tenement in the middle
of that empty vacant lot

all lit up at dusk
like some kind of
postmodern castle

but it was right around
christmas while nothing
felt better more intimate

on how to make it with a border agent
& turn around her interrogation
for a possible cup of coffee

that diner those off broadway
actors used to go to after a roll
call feeling grandiose & small

you pick up
your bucket
fried chicken

strolling in brooklyn
somewhere between
the dusk & evening

anonymous contented
beneath neon crosses
which read side to side

top to bottom
letters glowing
"jesus saves"

bullied boys
return home from
karate & bar-mitzvah lessons

vietnamese fishermen
come in for their
bundle of heroin

columbus brought over
the snickering caucasians
gunpowder disease religion

those puppet show people
return back to their portholes
in brooklyn for their discount

jugs of sangria
pleasantly passed-out
on their futons on the floor

listening to the throng
of distant foghorns
creeping up the alley

welcoming origami
ships from the old country
there's a sale on chicken wings

from the polish market
where wind-up widows
& all those young pretty

blonde girls make names
for themselves boogying
at the disco which is true

blue freedom
having absolutely
nothing to do with religion

amerika waz puttin
up awl those farm
o pseudo call cube

i calls in the hills
of portland
oregon

when the cops
came bust in to
take away yaw

best friend
amerikan indian
"montana slim"

on-the-run
from the
reservation

studying all day in library
taking landslide back
to broken hotel in hills

a reunion
of child
hood

thieves at the dairy cream
across from the cemetery
& wild whipping stream

clam rolls & onion rings
& *mr. softee* ice cream
makes life complete

being a young thief
eventually taught me
to be brutally honest

coming around full circle
not always a good thing
kinda leaves you lonely

always this weird obsessive
need to please but never liked
them getting too close to me

skinned knees
remaining peas
strolling home

through
the drizzle
along the sea

distant scent of chimneys
getting caught up
in my memories

always those overcast
skies during the holidays
sitting back in your mom's

cushy furniture
listening to old vinyls
ahmad jamal simon & garfunkel

finishing off hemingway's
"big two-hearted river"
sherwood anderson'

"winesburg, ohio"
observing that first
silent solitary snow

falling past your window
wondering what your first
love's doing what you'll do later

the slight footprints
of deer like a girl
you once loved

tiptoeing
through
the snow

of your backyard
disappearing back
into the bare woods

haunted inns get erected
from the dilapidated trees of
deep winding swamps & lagoons

grilled cheese & bacon
& rowboats clanking
in the marina. . .

the vacant motels
repainted pink
by the sea

the windy husks
of corn & wild
apple trees

bluebird
contemplating
in the drizzle

nothing means
more in the whole
wide world universe

two young girlfriends
sit on rocks chatting
by the wild currents

of a flooded river
behind the *super
stop & shop*

at the base
of the mountain
it's pumpkin season

the pink bubblegum buds
from the snowdrift crabapple
about to break open to white blossom

baby fast asleep
in crib to claps
of thunder

amazing will
never remember this
which is what makes

it all so memorable
beautiful & innocent
the thunder & torrents

& symphony of tree frogs
folklore all just played backwards
in a form of convenient amnesia

house grows
in the color
full roses

that rose with the broken
missing bottle & gorgeous torn
tablecloth at corner bistro in paris

where they buried
a quarter of jesus'
heart in sacre-coeur

the cobblestone cafe with nothing to do
all day but to dream the only thing
we had faith & believed in

chinatown rain
falling into neon
red rose puddle

thunder like the touch
on your shoulder
from a long-lost lover

a dozen
women in
a glass vase

love is simply
a language of
sweet-nothings

the only
thing worth
fighting for

when the unexploded missile
showed up all they did was lift
up the lid to reveal a bunch of

lost muted bridesmaids
looking out looking within
with their only request coffee

& cigarettes
& some broken
man to take care of

great big breakfast
of ham & eggs
at boxcar diner

purchasing
revolver
at reservoir

& following
the shoreline
all the way

to that quaint
motel overlooking
wild ocean smoking

homegrown
declaring love
promises & betrayal

the flowers have all shattered
in front of the blooming
traveling carnival

a house leans
up against a
ladder on fire

a town with not a single soul around
just steeples coming out the tops of trees
a forest with simply grandfather clocks ticking

wild wound-up cherubs kneeling by the stream.
on the outskirts at the coliseum tall thin
aristocratic women checking out

young boys playing
tennis on the clay courts
& like to teach them a thing

or two
about the
game of love

as the crow flies
right smack-dab in
to the medicine cabinet

for products & supplies
for the homosapien
to make life better

the tape recorder helps
us to memorize our part
of the haftorah & all the

reasons it took
roosevelt so long
to get us into europe

just send me off
to the palms
& i assure

you will return
a far better
man

monkeys can even
be swinging in
the background

wild tigers
sniffing at blue
gutters of sleepy

ghetto where natives
are still dreaming
beneath mountain

tin drums left
over from the
night before

missing floral umbrella
found tumbling around
radio station in the hills

i think we need
someone like
curl e stooge

for hour next
president
of thee

u knighted
states of
amerika

dreams of smooching
tomboy housekeeper
& going no further

she needs you
as much as
you need her

a home set
on a candle dish
in dripping universe

love fleeting
like a train
coming in

& leaving
the station
like that

instant
palpable
feeling you

get of the
imagination
& redemption

history's just that
staticky record spinning
forever never ever ending

all those things we
have a tendency
to forget—

jars of pickles
fermenting
beneath stairs

roadkill in the freezer
made with chili
sauce & beer

a whole row of red maples
streaked with sunlight
in the morning hills

brussel sprouts
still in the ground
harvested in november

ice fishermen
staggering home
beneath stars of winter

the hush of chimneys
always brings
us closer

chet baker with snowflakes
falling covering red bicycle
leaning up against maple

best thing about long winters
when birds like a miracle
suddenly reappear

right outside window;
little baby red cardinal
just sitting there in the

bare empty branches
keeping you company
your only companion

then just takes off
& vanishes when gets
sick of all the birdwatching

moose come down
from the mountain
into your backyard

wild apple rolls
off roof of barn
in the wind

what else
can you
ask for?

after those long impossible winters
those purple swollen rivers ramble
from the mountains into the village

where the puppetmaker
holds court along with
the hippies & lawyers

pretty young buxom women
collect specimens by the water
their knee-high rubber boots

& tight jeans make them
that much more attractive
then taking off with their

long nets
& buckets
to the mountains

the pale purple
lizard mist
blankets

& weaves in
& out the hills
of the forest

like the smoke
from ole time
silhouetted

skylines once
did when those
distant tugs came in

those weird wild
old time brick hotels
with long cobblestone

alleys that lead
to the lush hills
sound of bells

in the window
& downpour
of drizzle

stray dogs
roaming
the radio

tower & local news
which tells you "litterbug
convicted after lengthy investigation"

when i got that operation
& they removed my
internal organs they

found my heart
to be the shape
of an accordion

of an old blind woman
playing silent night
on the corner

of the french
quarter in
new orleans

rung-out roses
left on wrong
garden wall

where lamplighter
took off & never
seen from again

nowhere
general store at
the end of the world

being atop
the pyramids
masada at dawn

not much different
than reno n'orleans
in the ragtime morn

pedaling your bicycle
rickshaw past lost broke
down mansions to the ole

lonesome dead sea
mississippi shore
sacrificing it all

for some literal
radiant higher
than holy cause

the wild whipping spirits
you thankfully can't
get control

seeping into bones
like that stray
magnolia

the best thing
i learned in college
that staticky ole time

ragtime
radio station
on sunday

fats waller
ole satchmo
& jellyroll morton

metermaids mermaids
with the whole climate
change thing make out

on the rocky beach
don't give a shit
who sees them

casinos & felliniesque
buildings being put
up in the distance

suicidal seagulls go in for the kill
somewhere between the stern
& hull of the ship cuz just

got nothing better to do
with their existence
but to similarly

escape civilization
& start a whole
other reality

somewhere 'tween
discotheques
& the beach

vultures settle
in the palm trees
minding their business

while tourists
start up a
commotion

greedy
driven
ambitious

in the evening
girls ride on the
back of mopeds

in spandex & sequins
to murderous mansions
up in the corrupt mountains

mona lisa gives the weather
right where that wild temptress
frolicked in the fountain in *la dolce vita*

a seductive sicilian daughter
strolls on promenade
at sundown

you keep your shutters open
in montmartre listening
to french rap. . .

call it what
you want
call it kulture

when man first picked up
that conch shell &
put it to his ear

listening to
the echoes
of the ocean

for thousands of years
that skinny kid outside
the holiday inn in antigua

humble tired drained natives
hang out with their machetes
on the corner no complaining

contented
at the bus
stop at dusk

at the end of one's life get stuck
between chasing the dogs
& ice cream truck

i guess it's all
a matter how you look at it
best indian's at that *shell* station

the true-blue starving artists
used to always just settle
somewhere around

san francisco or paris
right around the mean-
spirited widows & thieves in action

the old retired con-artists having become
angry drunks hang out in bleak dark
bistros with very little left to offer

the cabana boys & leftover
housewives return back
to the shutters

the diplomats & out-of-work
actors not terribly
different

the opera houses & outhouses
of obnoxious sneering
pastors

you sell raffle
tickets for
your hanging

the stray dogs
& nymphomaniac daughters
what gives the town its character

II.

Denouement:

harlequins look out the bullet train windows
to orphanages and deep forests without trees
which eventually lead to the country and sea

where aristocratic loose ladies are having
cabanas put up by hard-working naive teens
who they relentlessly torture with futile inane

questions to desperately pathetically try to attract
attention—their husbands dead drunk passed-out at cafes
strays the most popular ones out here while the housekeepers

seductive sisters shaking out
the sheets on the sunny terrace
all displaced drifters in one form or another . . .

III.

Intermission:

they put up one of those burntdown rollercoasters
in honor of the hardworking blue-collar worker

i always preferred those mom & pop hospitals
like the small intimate one out in coney island.

after you got shot and they bandaged you up
for some strange reason asked you your religion

and told them you were jewish looking forward
before the sun rises to a bag of dried fruit & nuts

and quart of *old english* behind the
curtain of the boardwalk on the ocean

IV.

*Notes of an Expat: or simply
girls who drove you mad*

at dawn you go running
one sign reads *sicilia*
& the other *w. africa*

freaks doing vaudeville
in foreign languages
on the ferry

that very dramatic
tragic asian opera singer
& old stuffy men from sicily

poor brooding working girls
return home from the summer resort
old greek ladies play cards before the storm

you know you've reached your destination
when the firmament of milky fog begins
to melt off from the mythological island

where those morbidly-obese
twin brothers waddle out
of the belly of the ferry

aristocratic wives & husbands in sunglasses
don't speak a word to each other racing
their sports cars back to the suburbs

while see those dogs passed-out
beneath the palms of the polizia.
young smiling gigolos decked

out in military duds
with a whole life
ahead of them

V.

pretty young mothers breastfeed
their kin at clay court tournament

young girls barely break a sweat & clutch
each others hands at the end of the match

romantic boys keep the peace
engaged in their wet dreams

seductive sisters spit sunflower
seeds into each others hair

fathers in factories polish atom bombs

cars lit on fire most likely not a false alarm

vagabonds interrogated for blowing shofars
in cobblestone alleys which lead to the sea

welcoming committees of mean ancient women
keeping an eye out on strangers keeping down the
population planted on stoops with seething wolves

flamenco dancers living by the golden
rule of don't make me out the fool

old barbers place sunflowers in vases
while sharpening their razors &
wiping down espresso makers

neighbors they grew up with playfully pretend
to break chairs over each others heads on the corner
petty thieves & pastors take their morning stroll

foghorns welcoming mythological gods . . .

VI.
The Life & Times of the Conch Shell

when the running singing waves
say to the running singing babes
keep on always playing and
don't let anything ever get
in your way—that lovely
insane squawk of seagulls
and stray scent of the sea
all part of the same scene
all part of the same rhythm
and beat and sacred symphony
only come in when you're good
and ready—when mothers finally
call you in in their charming melodic
way at the end of the day while keep
the sand and sea on you as long as
you can in between webbed feet
and mussy hair with fresh bright
white sheets prepared and made
up by pretty giggling and gracious
sisters who grew up there; shower up

and all bronzed and handsome only put
on those neatly-ironed laid-out shorts
and short sleeve shirts at the end of
the bed and gobble up your feast of
fondue and schnitzel sitting on that
veranda overlooking the serene lake
sipping away from your glazed mug of
warm milk and freshly-baked shortbread
when the fishermen come sputtering in
getting their nets ready for the following
day with just the last clang of church bells
and shutters secretly shutting in the sandcastle
cathedrals at dusk, while know as a child even
a young adult, there's nothing in this world nothing
at all which can possibly ever stop you or once more get
in your way most of all your imagination and ability to be great

52

out-of-order divorcees show up to your door at dusk
mothers in the middle of a breakup never having felt
loved nor having an orgasm, while happy to be their
slut as temporarily makes you feel little less lonesome
& stick a message on your door *do not disturb, vacant*

"please don't take your munchausen out on me!"

53

only way to truly measure redwood trees
is how high they climb to the sky over tiny
donut shops in the rain after sunday matinees

picking up a bear claw & cup of coffee in the middle
of nowhere heading back over that industrial bridge to
the city to your sanctuary full of madmen & drag queens

54

first kisses in that forest behind the library . . .

forecast: horny, hot & heavy getting taken advantage
of to make her boyfriend angry having no idea how
much more man/ipulative was the female species

55

felt like whenever that pack of girls
showed up to your locker to tell you
she liked you you were instantly taken
hostage while what's that disorder where
you end up falling in love with your captor?

56

when school started in september
said you were gonna turn over
a new leaf & sat proudly eagerly
in the front seats then somehow
gradually in the end found your
self back there again (not exactly
sure how you got there) being a
wise ass in the mezzanine section

57

the misadventures of the misinterpreted

58

the crib notes to ancient civilization

59

the actors never quite made it . . .

60

puberty felt like that scene from "fast times at ridgemont high"
where that guy who just got dumped by his girlfriend forced
to take another job & still dressed in his captain hook outfit
after just delivering fish & chips to *ibm* shows up after school
to the pool in his backyard 'barely alive' asking his sister
& her to-die-for girlfriend in his dysthymic, down-in-
the-dump voice if they can possibly just keep it down

there was a very fine line between the mood
you constantly found yourself in & depression
& acting-out & intuition due to all those authority
figures so full of it & just naturally took back
everything they tried to so casually
conveniently steal from you . . .

61

was able to break down & figure out
complex proofs in a matter of minutes

62

resolutions & triangulations still feeling
completely empty, hollow & conflicted

63

passive-aggressive cuz constantly felt patronized
by flattery otherwise known as false accusations

64

how they didn't quite add up & follow the same
moral & ethical rules they tried to lay on you

65

how to handle a hypocrite (thief & liar & criminal)
how to be become self-destructive or (in)famous

66

how false/hoods in fact become the real accurate
truth(s) to an absurd & ridiculous existence

67

how this transcendent sixth sense became a lonesome
solitary confinement of both darkness & enlightenment

68

how you felt so much more alive a strange kind
of 'survival of the fittest' during periods of crisis

69

how you refused to take off jacket
due to chronic separation-anxiety
labeling you oppositional-defiant

70

how excessive masturbation turned all pain & pressure
into instant pleasure a panacea for the past present & future

71

the best thing back then was subtraction

72

fatal charm the remainder of false alarms

73

addition with all those little leftovers
lingering on top of pillars of math problems
which assured & promised you something for your future

74

sometimes just a slight hint of humor
helped to get you through the blues or
all that bullshit & mood they put you in

75

nightmares seeming something like both a prosecution
& character assassination interrogation & incarceration
while were just trying to get by in this existence
dreaming getting saved for the exact same reason
in the late late evening ghosts have the need
to get the last word in edgewise & you with
your convenient amnesia put on the stand
forced to separate the truth from the lie

76

*A Field Guide For Those Ole Time Child
Hood Games Played In Schoolyard*

Fig. #1

snap the whip object of game:

for one kid to grasp onto a tree while clasping
the hand of some other kid and go running like
crazy around that tree as fast as they can and
gets added on one by one by one by one until
the last one on the outside grabs the hand of
some other little man and you have a whole
line of wild hysterical children whipping each
other all around in the air holding on for dear life

Fig. #2

red rover object of game:

a team of children all line up across from each other
in field or schoolyard interlocking arms and forming a
human chain then one kid suddenly screams "red rover!
red rover! let ___ come over!" while identified child
takes deep breath and goes running like wild with great
gusto and vigor towards that opposing team across
the field and tries to break through human chain

if does so that team proves the victor
if not gets absorbed by other squad

Fig. #3

ringo levio object of game:

for one team to go hiding all over the grounds of schoolyard
then one kid suddenly shouts "ringo levio! 123! 123! 123!"
to alert opposing team they're coming and with adrenaline
flowing try to find each player on that team by tagging him
and hauling him to makeshift jail made up of team's children
with prison protected by a couple of other kids in case a kid
from opposing team wants to heroically go scuttling across
field avoiding being captured and freeing and saving whole
lot of them in an all-out every-man-for-himself jailbreak

Fig. #4

kickball object of game:

to be played very similar to baseball where each team
composed of first, second, third base, and shortstop
pitcher, catcher and outfield of left, right and center

while pitcher rolls big red rubber ball over blacktop
towards kid eagerly waiting for it to cross home
plate and kick the heck out of it then goes flying
(as if his life depended on it) in blue jeans and
flannel without opposing player catching it in
mid-air or throwing ball at him to get him out

Fig. #5

dodgeball object of game:

find a flat rock or stone and draw a long chalk-white line
right down the middle of asphalt where kids line up on each
side and toss that big red rubber ball at each other's bodies
and either catch it or get hit until all eventually boils down
to a couple lingering lost souls going back & forth
to determine who's the hero and who's the goat

Fig. #6

roofball object of game:

for the most part usually played one on one
with a tennis ball getting tossed all the way
to the top of slanted rooftop of school; if drops
once single twice double three times triple and
four times a homer where opposing players are
moving back and forth to try and catch for an out
scored exactly like baseball with the same amount
of innings—if ball gets stuck in gutter game over

Fig. #7

fungo object of game:

kid whacks ball with baseball bat
while a whole mess of kids hang out
in field trying to snatch it—whoever
catches it takes precise aim to roll it back
towards bat having been gently placed in grass

if he hits it he's up—

Fig. #8

king of the hill object of game:

making use of nimble imagination with military drills
trying to avoid getting tackled and taking a tumble or
spill to get all the way to the top of hill without getting
killed eventually declaring yourself the last lone hero

Fig. #9

freeze tag object of game:

kids go running arms & legs flailing
and if get tagged have to freeze up
right on the spot in the exact shape
and form in which they got touched

Fig. #10

spin the bottle object of game:

boys and girls huddle in quasi circle on asphalt
boy girl, boy girl, boy girl, and a boy or girl go in
center of circle and spin empty *coke* or *pepsi* bottle
on the ground and whichever opposite sex it points
to or lands on has to awkwardly, self-consciously
head over and plant kiss smack-dab right on lips

Fig. #11

truth or dare object of game:

self-explanatory exactly how it sounds where a boy or girl
ask them to reveal a very specific truth about themselves
usually taboo and forced to answer or a dare often of the
sexual nature which will eventually prove either a prude
or pervert and do things they definitely shouldn't be doing

Fig. #12

playing house object of game:

a true-blue battle of the sexes psychodynamic form
of acting-out where boys and girls are clustered in
cliques (going at it) taking on traits & characteristics,
role-play, and natural rapport of the male and female
in the grownup world for purposes of socialization or
literal 'survival of the fittest' somewhere between higher
than holy and humiliation seductive and being submissive

Fig. #13

flipping cards object of game:

each kid squats down hunched over across from
each other with a whole bunch of baseball cards
and flips them over on top of each other and if one
of the colors of the team on the bottom of baseball
card matches the other that kid gets to swipe
and pick up the whole pile of put-down cards
also to be noted another kid may rub their pal's
back with a good baseball player for good luck

Fig. #14

denouement object of games:

to return back to class with as much mud
or mother earth (maybe even couple rips
to your knees) on your canvas pants as
possible to prove your manhood point
and purpose and pride and deep down
do or die reason for 'living the life'

The Shortest Short Story Of All Time

on the first day of school he used to roam through that patch of pachysandra
down the side of his home & would simply open up his pencil case & fill it up
with brookwater finding this to be just as meaningful as any eraser or pencil or
ruler & on one of those miserable maddening days in school when the teacher
told the students just to put down their books & do something positive
& productive would once again unzip that pencil case like putting one
of those conch shells to your ear with the eternal transcendent echo
of the years & like some weird rebirth wipe down his eyes lips
nose knowing he had done something worthwhile in the world

Untitled

some of my best child
                    hood memories
were in the public library
and those little glass booths
where could have all the privacy
you wanted and not be bothered
and close the door behind you

and used to do extra reading
of like biographies on hemingway,
turgenev, crime and punishment

when i returned as a freshman
in college that really cute and
guess cool popular girl (whatever
the heck that means who used to
be pretty mean and intimidating)

now a senior in high school
flirting with you but what
else was i to do but being
something of a shy die
hard romantic (certain
sort of poetic justice)
savoring the moment
and storing it in
my files forever

Extracurricular Activities

the suburbs were best without all those promises
& blueprints & had a special on purple hightop
converses in the window of *buster browns*

while all the young boy hood babbling kleptomaniacs
met up at the babbling brook behind the shopping center
full of adrenaline attention-seeking totally unaware of it

Weather Report

i'm pavlov's dog seething
inside a brown paper lunch

bag feening for a dozen salt
bagels lox & cream cheese

blue-gray thunderstorms to be expected
while all you can do catch a double-feature

topped off with a fribble which
used to be called an awful awful

puddles outside the theater
& a whole life ahead of you

Ibid.

waiting for that spiritual rock
to be tossed through my window
with the message & all the answers

if not that at least a peanut butter & jelly sandwich . . .

Another Story Told

jesus christ gets pulled off the cross
(by who i'm still not exactly sure)
rolls his eyes like groucho marx
(another jew who suffered)

in a think bubble wonders
"never in all my days"
(man's psyche comes up
with some strange reason he'd
even have any interest in returning)
leo gorcey from the world-famous bowery boys
exclaims "over the river and i'll see you in the funnies!"
(seeming to make a whole heck of a lot more sense to me)

Good Night Everybody

the fact that we got 2 degree climate change
the fact that we now have all these massive
hurricanes cuz the whole damn gulf of mexico
practically too hot to swim in when the winds come in
the fact that the supreme court has now voted and cast
its opinion that it's ok to shoot someone on 5th avenue
and literally can be instantly absolved and bailed out
if you're president of the united states of amerika
the fact that we used to have that gimmick sensaround
when all your seats would suddenly shake up and down
during those movies "towering inferno" and "earthquake"
called "shake & bake" as all our dreams have come true
the fact that we no longer have *the donnie & marie hour*
while what the hell was the donnie & marie hour anyway?

Silent Film

home movies somewhere around 1970
5 years old at birthday party
with potbelly
great big dumb smile
& crown on your noggin

parents once said they used
to invite over neighbors for miles
around to watch me eat hamburgers

what a strange & bizarre image
as look back at your childhood
with a certain strange and keen
amount of happiness dread & nihilism

1973

1

it's all about traipsing through the fields
of dwarf pumpkins & dwarf watermelon
after literally reeling in bluefish all day
on the long island sound back to deck house
in the forest with best friend in cut-off blue
jeans around 7 years old long dirty-blonde hair
burnt shoulders & pretty hippy mother making
feast on screened-in porch in a field of fireflies

2

what else can be said & the worst that can be said
that dad a wealthy lawyer for the stones eventually
packed it all in & spent the rest of his days growing
out his beard walking shaggy dog stoned
in sunroom vegging-out to the later beatles

3

"yes i'm lonely! wanna die!"
while no matter how hard you try
all gonna hit you somewhere down the line

4

yet could never ever take away any of those images
those fields of dwarf pumpkins & dwarf watermelon
wandering home content with bluefish on our shoulder

No Substitute

that hippie
    teacher
        u had
            back in elementary
  who used to
read to us
        stories while we
            were all
                spread out
                    on the floor
      with her legs spread
           wide open
                to the world

& that see-thru
        underwear
            showing off
                that great big
                    hairy snatch
        below her
            plaid itchy dress
feeling engulfed
    & eaten up
               bewildered & lost
                    seduced & intimidated
                (guilt about seeing
something secret & forbidden)
                    even a bit
                      taken advantage of

              by such strange vague
      bizarre passive-aggressive
      behavior & seemed
                        to say it all back then
                              & the hole
                                im 'moral to the story'
            about relationships
                        between
                              boy & girl
                              man & woman

Things To Do And Not To Do With Your Downtime

1, look up old girlfriends & one-night stands

2, explore dreams deeper & deconstruct shallow fantasies

3, randomly put out dishes of chocolate kisses & weep hysterically

4, come to terms with all those mean-spirited kids & hypocrites
from childhood rsvp not necessary being the last holy link
to that chainletter after those unholy soulless cowards
deserted & abandoned for no apparent reason

5, take yourself hostage & make no demands
at last not so damn tough on yourself

6, plan to visit paris antigua andalucia once again
& this time cross the bridge to northern africa

7, be that wild hostile monkey stealing paella
from those spoiled obnoxious mothers & daughters
torturing young polite waiters just trying to feed their family

8, have tried every drug (no addiction)
try the last one opium the love potion

9, pick up every possible hitch hiker & figure out your purpose

10, finally follow through with putting up bowling alley
& chinese at last passed-out at the tiki bar
no longer bothered with "vacancy"

That Gas Station on the Corner of the Cornfield & Sea

life like some strange surreal story

of thieves & fairies

searching for the final prayer or punchline

death comes on way too quickly . . .

there is way too much focus put on the patrons
filing from the movie with their smalltalk talking
about plot & the players while so much more

should be put in the thunder & rainfall
& natural growth & development of
the real-life theater of the absurd

we exit the muted magnificent skyline
back to suburbia which holds a certain
type of silence like murder at a mausoleum

butterfly nets & badminton racquets
left on lush lawns with a pair
of binoculars hanging around

mailbox stuffed with junk mail
all proof of man but not so sure

On the Nature of Sport

1.

in those college football games
                    deep in the dakotas
   (between such teams
            like the bison vs jackrabbits)
i so much more prefer
            watching those pretty girls
    with pigtails
            & warm hearts & souls
                            running on
                    to the field
bending over
    broken bones
                    bringing them back to life
                            putting them back together again
    these are the ones
            i truly root for
                    & care about
                            & give a damn
& in my opinion
        deserve all the fanfare

2.

the spirit and soul is transcendent
even though at times feels like a hell of alot
of scar tissue to just eventually get back through

3.

people feel a more a part of the crowd
(& mob mentality) when they do
all that booing & hissing

has anyone ever thought of trading them?

4.

please tell me when it became hip and cool
for presidents to have to play golf and every
couple of months or so have to watch them
(and the secret service) out on the course?.
i think i'd have so much more respect if there
was just one who performed something like
synchronized swimming and like esther williams
see them in their swimming caps moving their
body parts back and forth to and fro looking
up gracefully to the heavens (from an aerial
view) as truly feel that would so much more
encapsulate and be indicative and relatable
to your everyday american. from what i heard
trump even cheats out on the golf course as
well (abusing and taking full advantage of those
so-called infamous winter rules) where if you've
ever played the links know that understood rule
to be a true test and measure of one's character
and honesty and integrity. to me i think i'd so much
more prefer someone who was an independent thinker
yet also passionate contributor to that classic old time
sport as well as forgotten art of synchronized swimming

5.

often those we try to
so desperately impress
are for causes (and effect)
and reasons completely opposite

6.

eventually at the end of one's life
man seems to suffer from all these
nightmares ironically coming from
the exact things was just barely
able to get through and survive

On the Nature of Split-Levels

1

may heaven be like one of those
great grand sleepovers with a little
room leftover to raid the kitchen

2

hell—jackie gleason
from *the honeymooners*
exclaiming convincingly
"i'm a' scared ! i'm a' scared!"

3

you'd do anything
for your wife & kid
like willie lohmann
doing his final bid

4

a note on your screen door reads–
"for the love of god, mow your lawn!"

Abstract:

they all seem so pathetic & self-important
in their sunglasses with their top-secret
phone calls over their cellphones like
maxwell smart from that sitcom "get
smart" but at least back then was some
humor making fun of the whole genre

I.

to think that raggedy
         andy all coiled
                  in my corner
& that rubber cement
         model airplane
              taking off
                      in my window
   of childhood
       would have
             as much influence
                  as anything else
                       in my present
                          day existence

to hope eventually
    to be discovered
        disheveled
            all bent over
                at my destination
      in paris,
          stockholm
turning down
    that award
        like jean-paul sartre

II.

how things can
    change so much
        in a day
so says
    the man
        on the ledge
            if only they
                were like
   bed bath & beyond
            exclaiming
                "your package has arrived!"
while most of man
    kind
    just
        playing games
            of hard to get
      mind games
          making you
            think twice
as never ever
      even
        crossed
           your
              mind

               having grown
                   for good
                       reason
so much more fond
      of inanimate objects

III.

my vision
    of a woman
        wuzz
            that jewish girl
                suzy goldberg
                            cute as a button
                      with that long straight
                  brown hair
          cascading
        over
     her new
found bosoms
                clutching her hand
                    rolling
                         round & round
           the gymnasium
returning back
      to school
          after the summer
              as if nothing
                  existed

IV.

   only request on deathbed
           some young puerto rican
                      removing brazier
      exposing those lovely
            olive skin bosoms

                    & might live
                        happily ever after
   with a sudden grin
       sweeping across
           face
              contented
                    like some seagull
                            with a wild wail
                                  at sunset
             at the edge
                of the ocean

what were those sticky pinocchio noses
that used to just hang off the end of those
suburban trees on the dead end of childhood?

Politiks

that very hip aloof arrogant chocolate shop i heard
is finally closing its doors due to the rumors of the
female owner "groping" her employees, not paying
them, and just glibly claiming "you gotta get with it"
ahh! those know-it-all liberals! but promise you never
ever will catch me being one of those prude republican
conservatives suppose guess why always been apolitical

On the Nature of Bluegrass

she used to live right by that river
where they made "deliverance"
then picked up & drove her
beat-up ole chevy to kentucky
with that simple blue license plate
& to make a living
carried power drill
& paint brushes
& gardening equipment
& fixed peoples' homes
& all that was ailing them
she was real cool & down-to-earth
as you thought whenever i bite the dust
might just bury me in a football helmet
like jack nicholson wore in "easy rider"
right around the mouth of the bronx river
my friend & i spent our whole childhood
searching for & never quite discovered
rolling through old men's backyards
through that pachysandra
those pals the only ones
who seemed down
& full of passion
& imagination
real & reliable
only ones
invited

On the Subject Matter of Separation-Anxiety

when i first got married i used to get these
sudden pangs of such deep acute separation
anxiety like the night before my wife might
visit (on a long weekend) mom in the bronx
and took her to the bus station in providence

and used to be so short and hostile and then
when i picked her up and she was sitting right
next to me would say such strange stuff like
"i miss you" and she'd respond "but i'm right
here" while if she only knew—if she only knew
(if i only knew always had this condition would
help to explain so much) while we headed back
to our nice cute quaint cape right on the lovely
laid-back bay in bristol, rhode island as i miss
so much those romantic days and all it did
for me and helped me so much to escape

On the Subject Matter of Racing Thoughts

whenever i suffer from racing thoughts
or major bouts of insomnia it's usually
to such sitcoms like "get smart" where
maxwell smart and agent 99 are involved
in some kind of bizarre shoot-out on a spinning
carousel with frankenstein and count dracula
while the finale usually ends up like life at
some wax museum surrounded by all your
family and friends not quite sure how any
of it ends as doze-off to some insane
infomercial like *monkey magnets* or
alien tape where psychotic white people
are manically taping up their cell phones
or paper towel dispenser or of course their
skulls inside some hard hat swinging from
the rafters but before you kick the bucket
know for some strange reason always had
a mad crush on agent 99 barbara feldon for all
those qualities and reasons why you love women
or those things in life you find it so hard to believe
in (and if believe in some higher being or spirit or

god they'll all show up anyway somewhere down
the line in some form or another on *the love boat)*

Just Like One Of Those Silent Home Movies

a large spanish woman working in her garden
naturally swallows me up. being the pest that
i am i go willingly as she heads back to her
pastel post world war ii kitchen to prepare
the pinata and bat and blindfolds for the
kids' birthday party who will all crazily
tumble in in their overalls and straw hats
and sandals and toys rapped perfectly in
polka-dotted wrapping paper and old
timers hobbling in with their canes
showing how they can also be used
for stickball and telling the same old
stories told a thousand times before
and how of course have absolutely
no regrets. everyone eventually returns
home and vanishes into thin air over those
railroad tracks and closed-down theaters
and dusty farmhouses fading with the
seasons behind laundromats and silos

Kurt Cobain

my wife and son take their
annual summer pilgrimage
for a couple days from
vermont to nyc to get
cultured on broadway
and asks me such
inane questions
like what's closer to *katz's*
little italy or central park.

i refuse to answer
but tell her after katz's
they can take a jaunt
a couple blocks north
up to where i used to live
on rivington all the way
to the east village and
st. marks place which
they've been to before.
i decide when they're gone
to turn myself into a big pile
of compost as have just gotten
so fucken sick of all the shit
of existence and craziness
of family life recently.
they're big with that shit
out here and just gonna
place myself in a pile right
by the barn for their return
home and hopefully it might
provide some kind of break
through and help to prove
how much she still truly
loves me while when they
begin to spread me all over
the perennials (the flowers
we picked up from the *von
trapps* which closed down
a little while ago due to the
pandemic) i'm gonna crack
some punchlines with my
wife apathetically respond-
ing "o, it's joey" and my kid
snickering in the background
and then end with a refrain of
kurt cobain hollering "gotta
find a way! a better way!

a better way!" unaware
he was the heart & soul
& totally without a doubt
the kind & sensitive one

Redux

when your wife goes
    on one of her summer
        pilgrimages
            with your kid
  a couple times a year
      to new york city
    good time
to catch up
    on those early
        james bonds movies
            planning your own
                personal one
                    to palm springs
    spending most of your time
        at one of those
           gigantic air-conditioned
              food emporiums
  reminiscing your child hood
        with tears streaming
            down your cheeks
having one time been
    one of those
        kleptomaniac thieves
            now brutally honest
  what it really means
to suffer like buddha

Little More Clarification

for some reason
    stealing those little
        chilly willy
            beer coolers
                for no particular reason
      when best friend
          whose father
              was a lawyer
would take me
    on trips
        with them
           so the siblings
                wouldn't kill each other
   cracking up
      when offering matzoh
           to the tourists
                stuck in sandtraps

Ambiance

during the holidays
    cozy up
        to ambient music
            from yule log
  in childhood
     u cozied up
        2 the
            ambient music
 from the vinyl
     soundtrack
        2 the original
           "planet of the apes"
              u got 4 hanukkah
    also loved
       the who, doors

                        & bob dylan
                            john travolta
                                stranded at the drive-in
    flicking on the switch
                to terry bloom's
                        divorced mother's
                            electric fire
                                place
            to get the ambiance
                        going
                            right by
                                bagel nosh
                                    & united nations
            in the upper east side
                            of manhattan
    waterbed salesmen
                    willie wonka
                    god bless amerika

Feels Like Zero

                    working that hotel clerk
                position
                    i swear
        at bed & breakfast
    right in the heart
    of hell's kitchen
                best part of it
                        being comforted
    with a sense
        of belonging
                watching
                        those
                            news
                                print
                                    pigeons
                                        purring

                thru fiery-lit
                            fogged-up
                                    alley
                        way window
                                who'd keep
                                        me company
                during lunch hour
                holy holiday
                        delicately
                        diligently
                        arranging
                        themselves
                         across the way
                                helping me
                                        to count down
                                                the days
                        (like our sacred national debt
                        going up by the second being
                        advertised on ticking billboard)
                                        balanced
                                            on the bleak
                                                        ledge
                of that anonymous
                advertising building
                                filthy flurries
                                        touching
                                            on the meaning
                                                        lessness
                                                            of time
                                                                & being
                        the old owner's wife
                                    breadcrumb curmudgeon
                                            stalking housekeeping
                making sure they weren't
                stealing soap & shampoo
                                you standing very still
                                true waiting to check in

          pharmaceutical families
from columbus, ohio
battle creek, michigan
          underdog missing
          herald square
          macy's, gimbals

That Garage Named After That Mafia Princess Wife

you remember when you used to hustle
that yellow, graveyard shift in manhattan
on 21st between 7th & 8th, back then the
statistic was like one cab driver getting
murdered once a week & having to slip
a 20 beneath the glass partition to the old
mafia dispatchers just to get a cab out &
those electric rolls of receipt paper u used
to literally used to take down notes &
observations & haiku of the mad
evening like silhouettes of hustlers
with their pool sticks huddled
in neon doorways old hasidim
hanging out with drag queens
in the meat market prostitutes
(sum of the best tippers cuz
knew what it was like to truly
suffer) literally kicking their
pimps out the back seat of your
moving taxi while opening the door
& completely unaware dragging them
trying to hold on through times square
things so constantly crazy & insane
your mind would go numb most likely
due to some sorta built up psychological
defense mechanism to keep you going

Much Better Than Any Those Smug Professors

some of my favorite heroes were people
like mickey mantle and marlon brando
who came from that area they like to
refer to as the southern plains and states
of nebraska and oklahoma—i also had
a good pal from there i worked with at
the bookstore in soho and eventually
became roommates when was getting
his doctorate at columbia and myself
my masters at yeshiva while didn't
spend too much time doing my
homework but just standing up
clattering away all day with my
typewriter up on top of an old
medical cabinet writing about
the blues and doldrums and
madness and philosophical
and psychological aphorisms
of mankind; living in washington
heights at dusk would pick up
fresh plantain and fry it up with
a couple cold bottles of cerveza
sitting down at that spare table
by the window with a transistor
listening to sports radio most
specifically the subway series
between the mets and yankees
hearing all day the crazy echo
of wild passionate dominicans
howling down the alley like some
kind of vibrant urban jungle then
gradually disappearing with the
evening and strange sudden silence
when they took off for the night back
to their apartments still sitting down

and contemplating life and these comical
kinds of ironies and cadences of the whole
wide world looking down to a lit alley window
and the simple solitary spare image of some
gorgeous radiant spanish mother and daughter
in their kitchen and at that exact moment knowing
and feeling all was good and calm in the universe

Vinyl

i wanna
    get in touch
        with those
            very very
old friends
    from
        adolescence
            way before
                any of the shit
                    of life
                        hit them
        no need
            to catch up
                on nothing
maybe
    just listen
        to good ole
            early
                neil young
    man
        he sure did
            have
                a way
                    with words

Sundays

yiddish paroxysms
a dozen fresh warm bagels
stuffed in brown paper bag
with lox & *temp-tee* cream cheese
the sunday times all washed down
with *brown cow* making this life
slightly bearable having to solve
those lovely logarithms & write
a report on that latin american
god quetzalcoatl putting it all
off to study the stat of every
yankee on the back of *topps*
baseball cards which seemed
just as relevant & profound
& a part of your reality &
existence as anything else
with tarzan & abbott & costello
playing on sunday morning television

Chemical Dependency (or the nature of ole past time)

i usually prefer the teams with losing records

most likely having to do with location

strange skylines fading into the heavens

or some ole forgotten city burnt down

wasted for some sociological reason

players you never heard of. . .

hearing just those 12 fans clapping

the alcoholics proudly nursing
their large watered-down beers

usually the best teams to doze-off to

and the most loyal you'll find anywhere . . .

brooklyn

a radio
    & leftover
        keg of beer
on the roof
    top
        of summer
            nursing
                here & there
    just as worth
        while
            as any ship coming
            in from foreign lands
    that italian joint
on cobblestone

Everything Must Go

everyone's a freakin' prognosticator these days
like some broken widow in brooklyn wasting away
with her layaway pawnshop crystal ball in the store
shop window bullshitting you and telling your future
i prefer one of those presidential candidates just simply
being an experienced butcher in their blood-stained
apron standing behind the podium cutting up some
german bologna cotto salami ny sirloin roast
shoulder and chicken thighs you can sprinkle

with garlic salt and soy sauce when watching
old humphrey bogart black & white film noir

The Rising Fall of Amerika

fumbling, we put up great kingdoms
while the coal trucks come rumbling in
eventually young girls will flash old men
in alleys as stray timber rolls downriver

birds whisper and cops in their tinted
vehicles secretly escort delinquents
down into the subterranean garage
beneath the courtroom to find

out their fate only touching
that much more on their
brutal and raw isolation
loneliness of existence

last image blood banks
and book stores and
brinks trucks rolling
slowly over bridges

The Amerikan Scream (protocol & nature of existentialism)

all those twister/tornado warnings (or the actual spirit
and energy) trigger the *frigidaire* to start blinking and
beeping madly—your wife finally after only a couple
months of constant breakdowns, blasts–"i've had it!"
and calls *home depot* ("where doers get more done")
and tell her since we bought it online there's nothing
that can be done but if want for some strange reason
to call frigidaire and have them call them back up and
make a report (the protocol) might expedite the problem

(completely delegitimizing the customer and like some
backwards postmodern descartes phenomenon prove you
'don't exist' or like camus want to put a bullet right in your
brain) who claim they followed up and ironically couldn't
get through at all (also too should take a video of the beeping
and get all those serial numbers). the tornado of course never
shows up while eventually like some reverse-parapsychological
physics *out of the clear blue sky* the refrigerator stops beeping
and get straight rain while i guess this is what they refer to as
the american dream—that infamous "great beacon," the greatest
democracy, or jean-paul sartre's brilliant 'clear and concise' existential
theories on freedom of what can possibly happen if have too much of it

Couple Tidbits:

I.

considering the nature and state of our everyday
horrible, half-crazed politics these days—tag
team dictators around the world, global warming
how you just miss those days when could just
throw one of those steaming warm washcloths
over your face after some great chinese meal
to cleanse and heal your aching heart & soul
with no need to come out at all chief meteorologist
looks like some version of eddie munster 16 years
old with microphone in the woods after the flood

II.

truth be told not sure why always cared
so much more about the single mother
realty agent with a chemical dependency
problem who feeds you such factoids to
look out more so for moose who will just
stand in the middle of the road at dusk and

let themselves get struck due to poor vision
as opposed to the asshole commuter or cop
(with an i-don't-give-a-fuck mentality)
responsible for taking them out . . .

III.

i wanna get seduced
by my tour guide

never really got her name

to me that's real culture

IV.

summer visitors who showed up—
a woodchuck from the woods my wife
keeps hollering at in cute voice "git! git!"
but feel bad for him just trying to make it
like the rest of us—gigantic black crows
bopping back & forth in their top hat and
tails wild turkey in their hightop sneakers
running down the hill of the orchard and
taking off stray moose who always seem
out of it trying to shake off a bad drunk
proud gargantuan deer with their newborn
doe shadowing them showing them how to
make it in the world that really cool laid-back
lesbian delivering grub feeling part of the family

V.

i live directly across from a community garden
and i guess those liberals planting their kale
are alright but think i prefer that nice and
kind suspicious bleached blonde who
brings her johns down to the river.
i never went as far as being a dope
addict but think if i was would just
shoot myself up and be the greatest
professor of all time (no matter the
interviewers never show up on time
while ironically i've always been
so punctual as deep down inside
resenting the fact that i'm the one
who has to make an impression)
black crows have arrived
and wish my wife knew
how much i loved her

VI.

your neighbor an old timer with a long white beard
and llama farm sells homegrown from his backyard
to pad his income—this more so is what i consider
the american dream; broken down cars and horses
getting delivered down the road with a distant echo
of them hammering up the carnival for the summer

VII.

nothing more brilliant & keen
than the change of seasons
subtle, dramatic, transcendent
& moving, overcast, bleeding
in the morning of brooklyn

& new orleans, holy, haunted
new england mill rivers frothing
in firmament rolling hysterically
historically past brooding and
melancholy solitary shadowy
red brick paper factories
alfred j. tickle company
the now you see 'em
now you don't cinemas
and ghostly boxcar diners
ole time cobblestone alleys
leading to multi-colored bales
of flaming mountains arousing
waking up those dormant emotions

ferry coming in from kanada . . .

On Self-Preservation or Self-Determination & Being Self-Sufficient

-1

after all the lights blow
out in the mountains
you catch up on your
reading & masturbation
like a leftover plate of
chickenbones & pour
in rootbeer in the rest
of the ice from your ice
coffee from *cumberland
farms* with that splash
of java & even feel
little sophisticated

before we moved into our home
out here the wife had nice little
signs like "bless this garden."
there were bullet casings found
all over the ground guess from
the husband shooting bottles
and on the top floor of the
barn *playboys* stashed
i suppose from son

and if this not
the amerikan
dream i don't
know what . . .

all those little
insurance agents
with their napoleonic
complexes on top of the hill

o

you blow boldly at your bear whistle
& god comes down from the mountain
going what's happenin'

as you continue with your head down to the ground
to bungee up the trash at the end of the driveway

when you get home you tuck yourself
into one of those pockets of a shrink
wrapped library book way overdue

snooze to your local cable their
protocol of protests & parades
all pretty much interchangeable

they've begun to put together
the rides for the summer fair
which will soon welcome all
the madmen & alcoholic fishermen
& delinquents & seductive daughters

the actors fast asleep on the train
coming in from the metropolis . . .

1

all those troubling dysfunctional
mansions on the edge of the lake

old money of love and hate

beach homes secretly tucked away
for kids of which they're ashamed
hoping to conveniently forget like
the wind and waves wasting away

teenagers who already betray

those wild vagabond thieves who are waiters
and know all the ins and outs at the majestic
opulent resort up in the mountains; wives
who are by themselves for the weekend

their husbands who no longer pay them
attention not so subtly try to seduce them
neighbors—old vindictive judges with
drinking problems having given up on man

mandated to go to the methadone clinic
after daughter serves her time in prison
while mom couldn't give a shit caring

more about her reputation and realty
agency and standing in the community

you wonder deep down inside who's the real criminal

it's usually almost always the repetition which kills you . . .

*Leaky black cat needs fix
ating raffle for flood relief
seeking blind man
for refrigerator repair
while local weather these
days just seems like some
bleak existential eternal
game of truth or dare*

like the kafkaesque nature
of our society and culture
has come down to when
used to be a social worker
for the boys' group homes
and shelters in providence
rhode island and a client i was
quite fond of who like myself
growing up couldn't stay out
of trouble and would every so
often take him to the mall where
suddenly out of nowhere just
spontaneously somersault right
down the escalator (shocking all
those obnoxious, privileged, and
entitled customers yet to me 'turned'
out pretty damn cathartic) and rip-off

those little golden good luck buddhas
while was so out there, deserted, and
abandoned but who was i (considering
my similar past 'at risk' background
of attention-seeking and acting-out)
to explain any the 'rights & wrongs'
law-abiding principles and all those
fucked-up, abusive contradictions
which put him there in the first place
with the primitive psychological
need to get it all out and escape

Living in Homeowner's Association Like Being an Animal in a Zoo...

1. having to follow those exact rules
2. always under a delusional control
3. wildlife caged & keeping the quota
4. don't feed the animals or may develop a motive
5. developing a weird higher-than-holy hierarchy
   (ironically herd mentality) & clique & culture
6. developing a very privileged underprivileged class of vultures
7. feeling like always under the microscope punitively watched
8. the difference between fact & fiction & paranoia & gossip
9. sexually repressed which may lead
10. acting-out or becoming dangerous
11. not necessarily loving thy neighbor but
    one-upping them & making an impression
    (this done in an absurd obsessive manner
    even if it means sacrificing your happiness)
12. sacrificing your family you claim all that matters
13. everything based on exact size & measurement
14. everything based on reputation & rhetoric
    until in a grotesque kafkaesque way
    become both tourist & prey...

On Safety

looking back at your youth it is always with a state of conflict and confusion
—all your supposed friends turning to snorting lines of cocaine not knowing
how alienated you ended up feeling so was it really so bad that you rebelled
turning to dostoevsky and turgenev; the french symbolists and existentialists
while during family get-togethers holing yourself up in your aunt's perfectly
neat immaculate bedroom with a plate full of fruit nut bread and ambrosia
watching the self-destructive losing new york mets on her tv set full of static
feeling so much more safe in that strange suburban green velvet castle away
from such relatives like that obnoxious arrogant psychiatrist who supposedly
at the end of the day made his wife get out his slippers while apparently real
stingy with the dollar and ironically left him for an economist and that phony
baloney whose dad passed on to him the plastic factory and would pretend
to earnestly ask you questions and when you started to sincerely answer
was already elsewhere—no wonder you felt so much more safe and secure
and could relate so much more to like raskolnikov or gregor samsa plunked
down there at the edge of my aunt's obsessively compulsive neat immaculate bed
with my ambrosia and fruit nut bread content watching those losing new york mets

One of Those Self-Starters

missing dog found on north street . . .

poor soul after my own heart . . .

used to take shots out there
at that bar afterschool on friday . . .

getting myself ready for college . . .

and a mini fridge full of *coors*
beer and dutch apple *pop tarts* . . .

compiling a solid 1.6 average . . .

just reading books off
other kids' syllabuses . . .

finding myself getting much smarter

Pass/Fail

i'm sorry but bukowski
    must never be read
        to like background
            new age music
like when in college
    & forced
        to have to
            take an elective
& thought why not
    might just try yoga
        to pick up
            some pretty
                young girl
or maybe if i get lucky
    even get laid
        but none of that
            ever happened
                & ended up
                    in the back row
all alone
    a lost romantic
        or something
            of a perv
trying to catch a sneak peak
    yet simply got
        the yoga teacher
            coming over
                helping me
                    to bend

　　　　my very inflexible bones
　　　　　　getting a passing grade
　　　　　　　　just barely hanging on

Higher Edukation

the comedians have all been
turned away from college campuses . . .

what a sad state of affairs

busy protesting
with their program
of political-correctness . . .

15 minutes of fame done over & over & over again . . .

the revolution will be televised on *youtube* & *instagram* . . .

you believe in the struggle but not one
where the kids don't even know themselves . . .

starving artists & brothers from the ghetto
who couldn't even afford a college education . . .

The Act of Sublimation

you wake up in the morning like an unfunny mel brooks
with your very bad arthritis going "oy! oy! oy! oy!"

you imagine deer leaping directly over the top of woods
flying across the heavens like one of those chagall gods

to places you never been to before like sardinia, corsica
although i heard it can get awfully crowded & hoity-toity

having memories of that older woman with the big massive bosoms
in bed with her in the morning on that summer lake in the berkshires

that beautiful tormented flat-chested red hair angel in that motel in maine

that blind date who exclaimed she used to be the best in her health club

that girl who said don't ever force me to make a decision between me & my dogs

that woman who claimed her & her girlfriends used to say if they
hadn't gotten laid for at least a year or so were like virgins all over again

that black girl from yonkers who'd only make love on the floor on rivington

that new divorcee from riverdale who came onto you from *wurzweiler
school of social work* confessing to me she had never had an orgasm
& like origami opening her up & after our internships coming
back to her apartment in sleepy hollow saying was gonna
start early spreading open her legs & started masturbating

all very viable options for arthritis . . .

77.

Skooling

a

your transitional object in childhood
was that little *zenith* radio playing
all that melodramatic bubblegum
rock & when the new york yankees
(when they had moxie & character
& didn't get paid a million bucks)
brawled the boston red sox . . .

that transistor radio said it all

b

getting it all out during recess a mad little hero
forgiven & forgotten in your favorite flannel with
mud caked all over the patches of cords gradually
turning to the holy sands of the spirit & imagination

b-

during childhood what a strange
lovely imaginary phase all those
fallen crabapples getting stored for
that much awaited rumored rumble
alas! no one ever shows up and you
remain a diehard romantic dreaming
of girls from the other side of the tracks

b+

all those swirling sacred scents
of the mud & grass & flowers
frontyards & backyards & the
mercurial miraculous change
of seasons subtly seeping
through the window taking
it all for granted but somehow
getting your adrenaline going
thieves of romance dreaming
of some secret escape mission
while being anywhere but there

c

Parent-Teecher Confrince

he takes a bite out teechers head n' leafs it on the corner of desk

a parent ly he's one of those badboys n' one of her faverites

n' during parent-teecher confrince she con fesses too mom

how she juss wants to run her feet threw his hair

times were much diffrent back then n' didant no what to make of it

way before that hole pile of polit call correck bullshit

so juss feels flattred n' bewild red n' returns too batman n' robin

when it was rekwired to take one of those utter lang widgets

d

The Collage Application

01 report card full of straight a's couple c's
02 was as passionate & loyal as they come
03 spent downtime in detention contemplating
the seasons magically changing in the window
04 was self-destructive for all the right reasons
05 believed in nothing but was a big believer
06 had a crush on my social studies teacher
07 knew all their personal lives
& why they despised their wives
08 hated being on those sports teams
& team comradery as just didn't feel
very much like a team

nor for that matter resembling
anything having to do with comradery
09 before they came up with such idiot
saying "extracurricular-activities" used
to love to read till lost all touch with reality
10 fell in love with the colorful changing leaves
at drizzly keg parties on the weekend as much
as anything else such as bs'ing with girls just
for my health stumbling home drunken finishing
off wine from the refrigerator & novels in front
of that great big window of river overflowing
11 did not look forward to the future or being
one of those upstanding citizens but retaining
my buzz as long as i could & holding onto every
thing i knew they'd eventually try to take from me
12 sunday morning with hangover
& feast of bagels finishing off
every section of *the times*
13 not exactly quite sure
or 'clear & concise' in what
i had to offer or what referred
to as "driven" & "goal-oriented"
with this psycho/social life & kulture

f

Manhood

got bar-mitzvahed but never felt
very much like a man—of course
had the man/dated disco with 'disco
disco duck & night fever night fever'
& the pogo stick contest & 3 piece
corduroy suit & jewfro but never
really ever got to that point in
my life where i felt what i guess
i was supposed to feel like like

i don't know maybe my freshman
year in college where i got laid by that
southern belle from the catholic school
across the way couple fish swimming
through murky fish tank listening to
grateful dead's *workingman's dead*

The Secret Life of Archie & Veronica

u never quite made it to bali
but at least had those glossy
catalogues sent to u in the mail
when secretly seeing that divorcee
trying to make it through *yeshiva*
to get your social work degree

while in all truth and reality
all any true-blue, red-blooded
all-amerikan male wants to see
is a sneak peek of a cheerleader's
pussy at some college game

where he may be reborn and
redeemed spending the rest
of his dying days being
a slave trying to live
up to her image

automatic sprinklers switch on
at dawn and heads out to give
the junkies their methadone

In Sickness & in Health

if u really
    luv your girl
        u also fall
            head
                over heels
            in luv
                with
                    awl
            dose
        cuts
& bruises
            on her
                knees
                      when she
                  suddenly
falls on
        the
           side
              walk
,
                go'in
                    flying
                        fur no
                            pawtickular
                              reason
      haven't
          grown
              up
                  haven't too
                      hide
                        behind
     hinges
         of halfway
              shut door
                  when her
                      parents

                            whir
                              go
                               ad
                                id
or hearing
        that harassing
                    quixotic
        chorus
            over
                    answer
                          ring
                              machine
        due
          2
                a cheating
                        absentee
                              father
    of
      "staying alive"

So Much Better Than Any That Jive

that old time black
& white noir had
such damn fine
storylines & style
always when like
a black cat crept
in with all that
cursed conflict
& crisis out of
nowhere came
a lit cigarette
& managed
to roll in all
these fancy

schmancy
bottles of
liquor where
instantly made
available some
sort of mixed
drink or highball.
when i dropped out
of college & took that
course to become a
bartender on 37th
& 11th ave we had
all these different
colored liquids
& little sponges
for the olives
while our teacher
would feed us such
factoids like 90% of
the drinks for customers
were highballs & thought
does that mean like 90%
of our lives we are in
some kind of crisis?
i did eventually pass
the final & got a diploma
but never a job as ironically
eventually ended up hustling
a cab graveyard way out there
on 39th & 11th ave. with these
israeli guys at least like the mafia
didn't charge me 20 dollars
just to get my yellow out
& while after 12 hours in
the madness of it all some
how at last found myself
empty & hollow satisfied

& content at the end of
my shift waiting forever
in the bleak desertion of
herald square just to get
that subway out to literally
"last exit in brooklyn" where
i lived at the end of the universe
coney island all feeling pretty damn noir

Evolution

    characters in order that they appeared . . .
        (no animals were harmed in the making of this film)

A Whole Other Sorta Survival of the Fittest

when you used to
    work as one
        of those reservationists
  in the hospitality
      business
                at the end
                    of your shift
     you'd still always
        manage
           to look up
              to the smoggy
                  firmament
                     of the heavens
    seeing that neon
      taper
       moving
             round & round & round
                  with all
      that constant eternal
        tragic

       catastrophic
        devastating
         international news
stock prices for
    coca-cola . . .
      ibm . . .
       disney . . .
        knowing all you
         could
          really do
   was head back
     down
      underground
       to the subway
     back to your
      brownstone
       in brooklyn
     that diner
      full of
       deserted
        leftover
         freaks
    picking up
     your
      cheeseburger
       & fries
bogie
 & bacall
    dead
     or alive

One of Those Love Letters Like the Leftover Fortune From the Crumbs of a Fortune Cookie

must admit used to have a bit of a crush on that beautiful blushing tomboy from brooklyn modest humble with all this natural charisma who used to terrorize the neighborhood & all those obnoxious coward stockbrokers coming up from the subway & her snapping "you got something to say?' ' & them saying nothing like god's light suddenly shining light on the schoolyard in the dim sun light of autumn & her just taking off on her rollerskates dreaming of one day making her mine (how i'd explain myself to her mom been cheated on way too many times) & a little later on climbing up the steps of our brownstone in the churchbells & foghorns & clotheslines & skyline going down at sundown over shipyard in our wall to wall linoleum apartment cracking up from punchlines after we made not-for-nothing sweet-nothing love . . .

Yeshiva

during that
stifling summer
in new york city
in between semesters
at *wurzweiler school
of social work* going
to that rich girl's
posh upper east side
doorman apartment
codependent daughter
who idolized her father
surgeon in michigan
claimed she was
a zionist but kinda
obnoxious & never
dated anyone from
718 area code
used to love

to get those
free samples
from *zabar's*
& just woof
them down
& toss her hair
over her head
like a super
model before
sat down for
a meal of bagels
lox & creamcheese
turned out in fact
was sexually frigid
& used to love to
speak porno &
tell you all about
her male cousin
from the kibbutz
who used to love
to walk around
her apartment
in his speedo
as if implying
would have
no problem
in you mimicking
that type of behavior
& had anything
could possibly
want but odd
couldn't help
feeling down
in the dumps
& deep down
inside constant
acute sense of

melon
cola
moreso
lonely
hollow
in between
her temper
tantrums
& declaring
her un
dying
love

Lenox Avenue

some of
the best
extra
reading
i ever did
was fried
rick nietzsche
outside that
highrise
project
in harlem
while
a social
worker
bringing
that old
black
woman
once a
month
her ssi

check
& one
of the
nicest
kindest
people
i had
ever
met who
sincerely
taught me
the little
things
in life
like
how
to be
humble
grateful
& show
respect
which
most
people
just
don't
get

Brunch of Idiots

ribbons of mist twist
through the mountain
when the snow starts
to fall—what else can
you ask for? that chinese
in portland oregon looking

over the willamette river
mai-tais & beaded curtains
with fellow thieves & delinquents
& nowhere to go like those ice
floes living at the *jack london*
donating your blood driving
a truck at dusk below that
volcano which blew its top

A Dozen & One Denouements:
That Ottoman Dick Van Dyke Used To Trip On

I.

i was never quite sure if your & dad's birthday fell on
the 20th & 21st or the 21st & 22nd or the 22nd & 23rd
so decided to just round it out and list all the numbers
from top to bottom and figure out the median which is
today and suppose if daddy is like somewhere in his
early 80's you must still be 29; something you used
to always playfully kid us about like some woman's
vain mason-dixon baseline which divided youth from
later life; like those days you might meditate with your
mantra (the only thing you had private from your off-
spring who were driving you crazy and up the wall) in
the white wicker rocker right below that low slanted
ceiling in your bedroom corner right next to that set
of coral curtains you ran behind on-the-run and tried
to escape from, desperate, overwhelmed, like some
demented game of hide & go seek and was forced to
eventually come out and reveal your identity guffawing
when you heard us searching and wondering out loud
"mom? mom? mom?" right next to that walk-in closet
every wife of a dentist dreamed of with your secret stash
of *joan & davids* which never seemed to get touched like
some museum exhibit collecting dust and that perfect suburban

1970's bathroom with that sort of sci-fi walk-in shower capsule
sloan gurney and i just stood in to try and see how high we could
get the water level; kind of chickened-out and took off past linen
closet in the hall where you hung john my stuffed animal gorilla
for chanukah past those stray succulent scents of pork chops
and baked apples and onions which penetrated the household
and right after supper at the bewitching hour after all your filthy
creatures had showered smelling of perfumes and powders
getting all our energy out running for our lives actually
feeling that palpable palpitating spirit turn to the here
and now ethereal imagination dashing through the lush
lawn (leaving little delicate dappled footprints) which
had already begun to spawn nocturnal droplets of
dew right before the whole world began to darken
and disappear and gradually go down on the horizon

Laughing Gas

II.

maybe i just got so used to sitting in the waiting room
of my dad's office, while always really hated or just felt
embarrassed or self-conscious by the preferential treatment
from those very sweet-speaking secretaries, as back then
kind of lacked self-esteem and guess just preferred those
sports illustrated and *highlights* magazines of escapism
yet one day after school not sure if i was seeing things
or just the mood i was in, or the long endless trip from
way out in the depressing suburbs we constantly took
with my mom religiously sticking in the exact same
8-track always played over and over and over again
of carly simon's *anticipation* (until played so many
damn times just waiting for the whole thing to end)
rattling over that insane awful industrial drawbridge
scaring the bejesus out of us, sounding like some
angry pissed-off dragon throwing his voice with
jaws wide open about to swallow us up past those

mysterious macabre blinking buildings like eery
monochromatic monstrous postmodern prisons
of concrete in coop city where you never saw
a single human being all the way eventually to
the pot of gold at the end of the rainbow over
there on utopia parkway, and suppose just
feeling all the stress and pressure of being in
this very competitive school system (causing
me to constantly act-out and get into trouble)
the expectations of the son of a dentist swear
i had seen goofus and gallant from highlights
magazine just suddenly showing up right there
on the spot on very clean mid-century furniture
with their polar-opposite personalities of mussy
hair and perfectly-groomed clothing and quasi-
moralistic values and self-righteous attitudes
consistently pitting one against the other–
"goofus is dirty and filthy; gallant is nice
and clean; goofus talks out of place and
gallant only speaks when spoken to"
while found was always able to relate
so much more to goofus and honestly
in the long-run just didn't get the whole
point of it, as always backfiring making
me feel so much more guilty and i had
done something wrong; johnny bench
and pete rose from *the big red machine*
just casually sitting there with dried-up
mud caked all over their uniforms and
their great big heroic handsome smiles
betty difazzio the nicest one of them all
whose husband was in organized crime
calling me in saying the hygienist will
see you now and me sidling in knowing
in the end she was gonna just whip out
that giant set of teeth and giant toothbrush
showing me all the parts i had missed like i didn't

already have enough on my plate, nodding-out once
again to the original sin anticipation at the bewitching hour

The Ancient Art of Dentistry

III.

what a strange
formal reality
the weather

living a life of leisure
that swashbuckling
sex symbol robert goulet

getting up
on stage
in vegas

belting one
for the ages
"i talk to the trees!"

seemed so much better
back then when
were alchies

& didn't even know it
1, 2, 3, 4 martinis
after work to calm

the nerves
staring out
10th floor

condo window
wife of a dentist
with a whole weird

existence ahead of her
excitedly quixotically
watching them put up

the whitestone bridge
like the ancient
coliseum

They Don't Make 'Em...

IV.

that old photo of my old charming
uncle arnold with a bald dome and
halo of cigar smoke literally swirling
over his yarmulka always seeming
to have one available some stubby
cigar jutting from his jaw always
so amicable always so aimable
with that great big humble
smile never ever quite knew
what he did for a living most
likely a bookie from brooklyn
with a transistor to each ear
one listening to the mets and
one to the yankees completely
content just crouched in that
corner at family get togethers
still with that eternal grin always
stuck to his face seeming to appreciate
and take nothing in this life for granted
while for a million and a half reasons
wish there were more around like him

The Fresh Air Fund

V.

1

skimming those pebbles along the lake
taking on a life of their own once taking
whole blessed long-gone life for granted

2

the distant echo of screen doors slamming

3

feasts of grilled cheese & bacon literally made by
ex-cons & alchies picked straight up off the bowery

4

pitchers of bug juice & the substitute lady carrying
her daily dose of styrofoam plates of peanut butter
& jelly for those sickly kids with very serious allergies

5

always wondered what happened
to those lingering remaining figures
in that human pyramid posing in home
movies on waterskis in the mountains
& thought nothing could ever come close
or equal that one rare brilliant blissful moment

6

ghost stories made up of our most fragile vulnerabilities

7

a trapdoor in the floor which connected dream to fantasy

8

all written in the rafters in graffiti for everybody to see

9

the daily symphony ping-pong harmonies of bullfrogs at dusk

10

sound of taps suddenly showing up
like some skipping record in the
form of static outside bunks

11

was it the moon or your racing thoughts?

12

fireflies or flashlights outside torn
screen windows keeping you up?

13

pulling those thin beat-up shades down
in the holy haunted hush of mountains

A Very Muddled Hx of Amerika

VI.

juancarlos stanton finally hit one out
(after constantly being on injured
reserve and striking out) getting
paid literally 25 million a year

ole time gangsters had the best looking carnations
like the hair color and texture of their mistresses
percentage of kids who made-out
to monster movies at the drive-in

news will tell you all about assassinations & genocide
& murder in the soviet union mideast & midwest
then switch to a commercial for instant spot
remover to take stains out of dresses

marvin webster "the human eraser"
found dead in a bathtub in tulsa

how come they never show the traveling carnival
returning home with the snoring lions & clowns &
cowboys with lassos in fetal position thumbs in mouth?

apparently they found some sort of ice glacier on mars
perhaps proving some sign of human life but looks more
like some scene from "the last picture show" or that opening
to "midnight cowboy" when they show that close-up of that
bleak & barren screen at the burnt-out drive-in movie theater

what was that period in american hx when they thought
it'd be classy to lay out that bright green miniature golf
carpet in your basement to prove a life of leisure?

preferred when they buried that very morbidly-obese
man in the piano cuz had nowhere else to put him
believe should have a costume party at one's funeral
as people are just so full of it with their lies & betrayal

real true-blue leftovers are those old timers
with drinking problems just sitting around
that exotic bar at the chinese restaurant

looking like buddhas always pissed-off
blue & down in the dumps when the young
content couples come in with members from
the methadone clinic and motorcycle club

The Zoning Board

VII.

Phaze 1

a multicolor array
of pick-up stick trees

Phaze 2

when no one's looking
completely eliminated

Phaze 3

sociological postmodern phenomenon
of leaving pure bare naked mountains

Phaze 4

newly man-made manufactured immaculate
suburbs set up on stilts alongside the highway

Phaze 5

clusters of cookiecutter condominiums which all
look exactly the same while never see anyone
out there—exactly how it was planned

Phaze 6

visions of *home depots* miniature golf
chinese buffet & bowling alleys

Phaze 7

newspapers only get delivered
now in the wee hours of the night
by angry old men still on probation
not giving a shit where they drop 'em
somewhere destined between beat-up
farms with vicious snapping guard dogs
& suddenly crossing that boundary to shangrila
of perfectly manicured dead end mcmansions

Phaze 8

the only signs of life
automatic sprinklers
going on exactly
at dusk & dawn

Phaze 9

plaques of american indians in loincloths
& the year it was discovered when
enter new quaint towns & villages

Phaze 10

don't even need your hand
on the wheel of your luxury
vehicle when tearing through
tumbleweed tornadoes & bison

Phaze 11

a whole line of massive billboards which read
such things like "ban bullfighting" when you take
your air-conditioned journey through the great amerikan
desert & reach your off-season lewis & clark postcard destination

Phaze 12

best western where you get your
free breakfast of coffee & danish
somewhere on the schmaltzy strip
out in palm springs where the late
great tv personality johnny carson

once lived on that estate measured
only in 1000's of square feet &
amount of wives he accumulated
supposedly dying a very lonely man
just like elvis without a single soul around

A Sci-Fi Kinda Reality Show

VIII.

Part I

1.

we now got poor stormy daniels
who can't anymore get johns
cuz of her past life
with the donald
scaring off
future clients

dampening dream
of that nest egg
down in the sun
shine state of florida

now gotta go food shopping
like the rest of us at places
like *piggly wiggly* looking
for sales on german bologna
industrial size chock-full o' nuts
ritz bitz and hungry man dinners

2.

in amerika taylor swift
has become a product
like *wrigley's chewing*
gum & *coca-cola*
who was it back
in the day who
had her legs insured
for a million bucks
right around when
poor marilyn monroe
was overseas with bob
hope, as he exclaimed
to the troops & a return
roar "i want to show you
what we're fighting for"

3.

we seem to have conveniently forgotten about
the greats like jimmy stewart james dean marlon
brando & now got the 20th sequel to rocky balboa

4.

the great sci-fi classic 'planet of the apes'
50 years later going into its 50th version
now all just computer-generated set up
simply for confrontation & special effects
("in a theater near you" then streaming
then blu-ray then going directly to dvd)

5.

amerika's got all these awful horror films
well how about at like 3:43 in the morning
when suffering from a bout of insomnia
somewhere between the constant instant
replays & slow-motion assassinations
just turning the channel to the flowers

6.

everything's come around perfectly full circle
while once again got rich kid college protesters
who got nothing else to do with their free time
(if they get arrested might even look nice on
their "activist" resume) while never once know
what it's truly like to be hungry or to suffer

i even remember once where this aloof obnoxious
self-righteous daughter showed up early before other
protestors & opened up her *ll bean* chair scrolling on
her smartphone & ordered & had delivered take-out
sushi right there on the spot like some classic form of
privilege & entitlement or even ironically gentrification

7.

been a bit concerned these days
gonna be reincarnated as mr. roper

Part II

madonna to give free concert day before apocalypse . . .

noticeable sharp gains in stock prices for . . .

tiny homes
hard seltzer
keurig dr. pepper
medical masks
kleenex
disney

distant dogs bay in the breeze. . .

world federated wrestling bobblehead dolls
bob out of control in kitchen windowsills . . .

tsunami warning in the philippines . . .

baseball season to be postponed until further notice . . .

meteorologists hunkered down in the keys . . .

feels like 73 degrees at hero's general store . . .

tornado chasers in amerika's heartland . . .

factoid: madonna psych hx picking up young latino boys in her limo
    in the lower east side right around *vasack's drinking tavern*
    where the old timers and independent actors go to die . . .

Wildlife

IX.

and so at the final destination
grand illusion you got women
of all different shapes & sizes
part exhibitionist part self-conscious
just standing in the ocean repetitively
hitting their paddle balls back & forth
in front of those shimmering miraculous
metropolises oil tankers & suntan lotion
& the same old issues with boyfriends just
trying to keep them happy (virtual impossibility
considering all of that nihilistic worrying) grand
existential question of their own mortality which seems
like some really deep shallow version of the tourism industry

The Existential Collective Unconscious

X.

i'm not making this up but i swear every couple decades or so
there are these real-life true stories about people who have to
be rescued at the bottom of the sea usually somewhere right
in the midst of the stifling summer—for me, it was a couple
decades or so ago and had just broken up with some crazy girl
from *wurzweiler school of social work* at yeshiva who proved
just not to give a damn, while for a summer job, a former ghost
of myself, and just going through the motions, ended up being
a front desk clerk at *the murray hill suites* nightshift in the city
and it was a team of russian sailors and felt really bad for them
if they ever were gonna save them, while simultaneously feeling
numb for a number of different reasons, and with the couple of
bucks i saved just took off at the time to italy and remember taking
this ferry from naples to sicily and being all by my lonesome, brooding,
fixating getting pretty freaked out by the concept and notion of being

at the bottom of this ship, and if i never made it, no one would ever
know (and would anyone really care or give a damn) and how much
that touched on the erratic nature and absurdity of my mortality
eventually like a dream making it to the misty shores of sicily.
now apparently right around the exact same period of summer
approximately 30 years later for completely different reasons
they got these wealthy tourists who decided they wanted to
just tempt fate and explore the remains of the titanic and similarly
got lost and stuck down there, and we're having to once again try
to find and save them all the way at the bottom and deepest depths
of the ocean while strangely, obscurely find myself feeling a similar
sensation and feeling of being 'lost and numb' yet for completely
different reasons and if i'm still gonna ever make it and would
that even matter much nor make much of a difference?

Shipping Logue:

take nighttime ferry from naples to sicily not caring
if you make it back dead or alive not sure if you're
dead or alive after a bad breakup with a manic girl
with borderline and ship full of aristocrats burlesque
acts lonesome young women returning back to their
native land after working summer resorts amateur
opera singers and old timers passed-out on deck
as if fantasizing about forbidden daughters next
door where their widows play cards having accepted
their station in life while you always wake up bleary
eyed not quite sure where you are suddenly seeing
through the milky fog that miraculous island rising
from the misty mediterranean and hail a taxi whisking
you past the early morning old broken down mansions
and mountains of wicked wasted wilted palms to palermo

The Opposite Sex

XI.

i remember when i used to live with that much older southern belle
down in the west village who worked at *pierre-deux* on lexington
and on some fine summer's day all of a sudden finding myself
without a penny to my name wasted drained in my marlon
brando leather cap dropping in to ask her if i could borrow
a couple bucks and miraculously found she didn't even
get pissed-off as if showing off this much younger bad
boy who was there to protect and save her from all those
people and things in life that had tragically betrayed and
lied and let her down while like some kind of mad coquettish
blanche dubois used to casually take off her shirt and bra and
just ask me to turn around knowing exactly what she was doing
and going down (with the obsessive need to turn me on from an
ex-boyfriend who had cheated on her with a much younger woman)
as i saw her completely naked revealing those tiny fragile champagne
cup bosoms as a distant reflection in that smudged dusty antique mirror

Fragmentations

XII.

i

june
say
pa
may
b
inn
thee
end
waz
juss

dat
ole
time
squirt
dink
car
nation
witch
broke
down
loose
ing
itz
will
2
go
on

ii

u
never
  once
calm
  planed
    like
     1
those
  priddy
    red
scar
  let
    leaves
      blow
    wing
   off
     skull

```
        ton
     brand
  jizz
      at
        end
          of
     awe
dumb
```

iii

Wake
king
up
inn
mourning
all ways
wit no
1 no
wing
u'd
never
give up
just thee
way u
were
razed
stow
wick
&
strong
new
no betta
in the brilliant
impoverished
ram

shackle
rag
time
mansions
of dawn
those
mag
noll
ya
muz
o
leums
awful
awe
full
o
spirit
&
soul
slow
ray-
d-
o
mission
district
magazine
street
mississippi
river
of witch
waz never
ever any
returning
home

iv

the heartest
part of the day
as a runaway
was right
around
dusk
trying
2 figure
out what
yewd dew
with the rest
of da night
realizing u
were so alone
so faraway
from your
home what
the hell
u were
doing inn
frisco reno
in that broken
glass hobo
burlington
northern
motel
at the end
of the tracks
that number
u took down
frum dat
lawn
dro
mat

v

at
seasick
sod farm
tick tock
of ole
broken
down
clock
tower
e
fem
in
ate
vag
a
bond
hustler
wit
poor
ragged
son
trying
2 sell
u shiny
tarnished
watch
soul
pawn
shop
bones
on
da
way
2
creaking

floor
boards
of
heaven

vi

yaw
united
states
amerika
were
awl
those
missing
in aktion
pieces
frum
dat
jig
saw
puzzle
awl
those
action
adventures
as a jung
runaway
eventually
putting them
awl back
2gether
on that
motel
wall
wit

dat
budiful
redhead
girl & pink
bedspread
& glow in
the dark
western

vii

you
finally
at last
get to
your
dusty
nation
having
thought
it'd b
soo
much
better
now
lost
be
tween
reality
&
illusion
&
can
see
why
fiddler

brando
birdman
of alcatraz
took 2
thee
starry
heavens

Freedom

XIII.

after all that suffering
all those long journeys
does not one deserve to
be just a little bit happy?
i can't begin to tell you
how good paris looked
20, 30 years later like
some endless glowing
kingdom of the imagination
how much more appreciative
receptive and grateful—
the senses so much more
alive sharpened and keen
gare de lyon train station
in the morning empty
and clean haunted holy
and taking off on the *tgv*
finally all by my lonesome
to the brilliant blue beaming
mediterranean of nice when
the palm trees just suddenly
show up out of nowhere like
some miracle or dream just
sitting there alas in the
anonymity of the beach

happily not knowing
a living breathing soul
in my wrinkled linen suit
eating my shrimp and linguine
reflecting and in this reality literally
seeing my whole life pass in front me

78

"i don't know what to believe!"
is where almost all philosophies
naturally stem and spring from

79

people are so phony and full of it in this world
and eventually just seem like a hole hell of alot
of junk mail, while the build-up and repetition
just always made you feel so alone not giving
a damn about that metaphor if a tree falls in
the forest or not, as your supervisor at the
mental health clinic who constantly breaks
confidences and talks behind clinicians backs
says we gotta one day get the wives together
and my first thoughts, hope i'm not included

Case Study #1

i remember when used to be a social worker
waiting every morning in principal's office
for my clients and this mother who would
always show up out of breath with her kid's
clarinet telling the secretaries sorry he forgot
it while they very respectfully humbly would smile

(from this repetitive ritual) subliminally understanding
the unconditional love of a lovely mother for her child

Case Study #2

that vice principal with the reputation
of screaming and hollering at the kids
sent into his office as if this was supposed
to be some sort of tough love dickensian
discipline only really retraumatizing
them and making them regulars

Case Study #3

that client our first session with his mom
bragging how he had been through 5 or 6
therapists and i'd be the 7th completely
unaware i was exactly like him as a kid
and relished the challenge eventually
having him gabbing up a storm at least
giving him some chance in this world

Case Study #4

all those days as a child constantly getting into trouble
while remember my fellow delinquents used to with love
and respect mention as a means of support felt like your
whole world was coming to an end wondering why you
would do such wild crazy shit and it almost becoming
something of a humbling religious experience realizing
i had absolutely no bad intentions nor a mean bone in my
body and if i can just somehow possibly get through this one
they'll one day deep down inside know me for the guy i really am

Case Study #5

working the boy's shelters in providence, rhode island
running the anger management groups resentful that
they even had to be there in the first place due to
some form of parental neglect or abuse and this boy
just bursting out loud "place smells like straight ass!"
while i instantly retorted "smells like ass or straight ass?"
which right away cracked them up and made them hysterical
which is what you call a "breakthrough" (in a certain sort of
distorted way developing trust and able to connect and relate to)
with kids who have been lied to and shitted on most of their lives

Case Study #6

looking way back when to 5,6,7
there were no better expressions
no better action & adventure
no better spirit & imagination

Case Study #7

david birnbaum rolling sushi in his basement
yourself as a child suffering from a case of
kleptomania of constant attention-seeking
"trouble always seems to find me" one of
those self-fulfilling prophecies of some
deranged jesus hanging on the cross like
one of those wishbones licked clean to the
bone by a stray dog from beneath the boardwalk

Case Study #8

i remember those daze out in brooklyn
sometimes working 2 to 3 jobs at a time
hustling a yellow graveyard delivering pizza
for *pizzeria uno* on 6th avenue in manhattan
on a bike and suddenly seeing that guy leroy
from the movie "fame" just sitting at the bar
neither a good nor bad drunk just real low
down and down in the dumps and knew
right there at that moment could take
absolutely nothing in this life for granted
like those 15 minutes of fame (kinda ironic)
no different than if a tree falls in the forest

Case Study #9

returning home bloodshot brokedown dead to the world
in bumpadabumpa just to get on the highway to a wife and
newborn i loved more than life itself with a brand new pair of
infant overalls from the mall and coconut shrimp from that 99 pub

Case Study #10

keeping an eye out on your kid
you fall asleep in the children's
section of the library during the
thunderstorm with all those leaves
fallen on the front lawn across from
the old victorians and sweet aroma of chimney
smoke somewhere between the river & mountains
steeples set back—sprouting from the drizzly trees
& teenagers hitchhiking as long as you'll take them

80

a whole other lifetime ago—

bucky dent thurman munson goose gossage
clattering in the spokes of your bicycle

the sacred seasons just over your shoulder

81

that milkman who you never met
or saw like god or santa claus
with those morning bottles
glazed in dew suddenly
showing up fresh and
filled up left at the door
of your backyard porch

82

we got more accomplished
on the lush lawns of childhood
where a real good full day got put in

practically experiencing
& going through
every emotion

never underestimate or take
for granted the imagination
& promises made to friends

our version of heaven was that schmaltzy
music played in that flickering lounge down in
key biscayne, florida & a whole life to look forward to

god coming through
the clouds every morning
like a boy shooting marbles

83

living in that shattered snowglobe with
it always falling down an inside job
looking in but also looking out

84

that snow constantly
falling down jackie
gleason the great
one finally at last
no longer "i'm a
scared! i'm a
scared!" all
is calm all is
bright church
bells & fog
horns pro
vide finest
confession
of all time
while those
old time
brownstones
of brooklyn
with not a
single soul
around
silence

85

that one winter vacation
as a freshman in high
school reading all of
marx's communist
manifesto richard
wright's native son
& huckleberry
finn in front of
that roaring
blazing fire
with cross
country skis
leaned up
against
natural stone
hearth & the
natural fragrant
scent of ski wax
& gorp made out
of dried fruit &
chocolate & nuts
at the *mountaintop inn*
in vermont never seen
snow come down like
that or build up like
that feeling transported
to a whole other ethereal
lost & radiant world skiing
down that small hill from
the inn straight into the forest
cross country skiing silently
with my sister quiet escapist
pleasantly wild safe & secure

86

studying album covers was pure escapism
picturing whole other realities & existences
in my opinion was a certain sort of
human growth & development

when feeling stagnated going shoplifting
loving the challenge ironically leaving
the album "hooligans" on the bus
i guess feeling guilt-ridden

87

waiting in the early evening (mother
consistently tardy) to be picked up
outside the y bloodshot & shivering
outside the synagogue cause required
for bar-mitzvah wondering if this was
what it was like to be a man feeling
eternally deserted & abandoned

88

that tradition & custom where some door
was left open for elijah while felt like

the beginning of the welcoming
of ghosts & phantoms...

who were you gonna be for purim & passover?
haman? raskolnikov? old man goriot?

the lawnmowers starting up
leaving a trail of echoes at dusk...

89

always wondered if those local commuters
had died years ago would anyone know?
always wondered if they were alive
there'd be a similar outcome?
always wondered if that young strong
muscleman tickettaker was the father
figure we never had & all those opaque
pasty passengers simply dysfunctional
family members who didn't give
a damn if you were alive or dead?
always wondered if those punched tickets
right over their heads proved they existed?
always wondered if they bleed & weep & scream & cum?
always wondered if that rum & coke might allow them to cope?
always wondered about those passed-out party girls who looked
more like fallen angels from the nightclub & if they ever made
it back to their safe & secure daddy's little girl midnight homes?
always wondered who were the real heroes & villains in this
faceless exodus back to the stillness of deathly-silent suburbia?
always wondered with all those briefcases & newspapers
while world already torn into a hundred-million pieces
would cause their eyes to at last finally open & get it?
always wondered about that absurd, mean-spirited
aggressive custom of snapping & folding the paper
(like the opposite of an origami artist with no
imagination) sexless soulless with no manners
or etiquette as if no one else existed around
them & will even go so far as to pathetically
rip it so no one else can possibly get to it?
always wondered if they were on one of those
top-secret cellphone calls would finally 'get through'
& one day just learn to not be so self-important
& self-absorbed & get a clue or creative bone?
always wondered if they were just visiting jail
'do not pass go, do not collect two-hundred' would

inspire them to get out of the mental prison they're in?
always wondered if like some sort of plato parable
& them just looking out into fleeting silhouetted shadows
from deep dark windows would anything at last exist at all?
always wondered if their delusions ever meet 'the illusion'?
always wondered how all truths lied in desolate emptiness
of ticket booths & telephone booths transporting you
away from all forms of brooding & the blues?
always wondered when they at last pay their dews
& pay off their mort/gauge become new men or just
broken down superheroes not being able to get out of
the routine & ritual & decide to go into work just a little
bit later & work less hours? always wondered if the commuter
afraid of his own shadow ever really gets back home to where it all started?

90

Parable 1

after you return home from college
there is a certain surreal silence
you can't quite make out while
your house seems like a museum
of past characters who play roles
simply going through the motions
you no longer know what about along
with silhouettes and shadows especially
at closing time during the nocturnal hours

Parable 2

reality becomes walking out the dark theater
bleary-eyed, brooding, into the bright, beaming
sun through puddles after an apparent rainstorm
not really caring or giving a damn what is what
this becomes the metaphor for 'mixed feelings'

your being taking in all these brand new forms—
the spare simple sound of swollen rivers, scent of
mud & magnolia & glistening sidewalks & homes

Parable 3

sharing your fried chicken bones
with those watch dogs at the used
car lot in red hook looking to
the statue of liberty in harbor
during some silent snowfall
is the rise & fall of civilization
at last with no one to speak of

Parable 4

those placid white condominiums
of the suburbs looking over the duck
pond, streaming white noise of cars
on the highway and throbbing trains
in the distance triggers you to look back
with a sense of sentiment, nihilism & nostalgia
while nothing quite equals the language of love

Parable 5

backed in the corner by life
she did the best she could
and was a good sport and
looking back that's all that
can be asked for and in
my opinion in mind body
spirit and soul what love is

Parable 6

i don't know—sometimes i just view life
as not just christ on the cross dying for
us all but all those people who just stood
idly by knowing all the sacrifices he made
in trying to guide and give us a better life

Parable 7

freedom is just
a feeling that lasts so long
while never take it for granted
cuz before you know it it'll be gone

Parable 8

don't listen to you anyway
so write for the masses if
you know what i'm saying

spend my days in that great big
aluminum siding horse of troy
joys of poetry & philosophy

while outside they hammer
and whittle away as it's all
futile and simply a repeat

of the brutality
of human nature
war and religion

the hotel clerk bickering
with the rich spoiled
girls from europe

Parable 9

o! the idealism of youth
no period of more
beauty or truth

Parable 10

those insane liberating
childhood games like
crack-the-whip ringo
levio 1,2,3 1,2,3
if similarly later
on in reality we only
had as much resilience
and strength of conviction
as this too holds as much wisdom

91

most substitute all their pain and suffering
into self-imposed crises and drama as opposed
to considering a humanistic type of sublimation
transferring it to romance and love taking in all
the keen shapes and forms and world around them

92

if we never give up
i do believe we get
tougher & stronger
but perhaps
just a little
more fragile
& sentimental

& in need of hugs
& kisses & spooned
with tea & crumpets
by the light of bogie
& bacall or was that
tracy & hepburn
who all experienced
their fair share of loss

93

if only we made the effort to more concretely
define language as opposed to language defining us
prejudice pre-judas passing instant judgment
with way too much jealousy & pettiness

herodotus was leftover erotica . . .

94

wittgenstein very similar to nietzsche
in their [obsessive] nature whose keen
social observations & 'interrogations'
pretty accurate but still ended rather
lonesome & isolated in the madness
of the beauty of the alpine mountains

95

so many great scholars
have something of a silly
slapstick sense of humor
as if needing some kind
of punchline (instant-gratification
or cathartic release) after all that time

devoted to the proclamations & proof(s)
(& counterarguments) of a rather absurd life

96

every great writer becomes something of a savior and has no idea
what you're talking about when you ask them so says hemingway
was just trying to write a good story when awarded the nobel prize
for literature for "the old man and the sea" eventually couldn't save
himself and put a bullet in his head (the paranoia and melancholia
drinking and all those falls took their toll damaging the brain) while
so many writers went the same way tennessee williams jean genet

joe dimaggio requested the gravediggers who worked
at the cemetery to leave a rose everyday by marilyn
monroe's grave—for me it would simply be a salt bagel
small carton of *brown cow* and annual donation to the union
of dummy-ventriloquists hopefully the ones giving my eulogy

97

we originally get motivated & inspired
by the concept, sensibility & aesthetic
while comes by no coincidence goes
all the way back to our instinctive
primal interests, dreams, fantasies
& traits & characteristics from our
identity exhibited in early-childhood

Proof 1:

listening to the musicality (lyricism) of the toddler
one can practically fathom (& deconstruct)
the derivation of human language

Proof 2:

all that 'stuff' as a kid which was supposed
to make you "well-adjusted" in fact backfired
and ironically did the opposite considering all
the anxiety it provoked (focus on performance)
and forced unconscious boundaries and structures

Proof 3:

as far back as i can remember
always keenly sympathetic
but strangely enough
not treating myself
with a whole heck
of a lot of respect
nor able to
keep myself
out of trouble

Proof 4:

always got along so much better
with the "fallen angel" (on an
intellectual & intimate level)

Proof 5:

it's people that make you lonely
& hunger for strangers to relieve
you of such empty absurd realities

Proof 6:

it's the subtlest of fantasy
which leads to mythology
when in real time of need

98

our cultural & topographical landscape
can bring about a sense of situational
depression even making us numb
take for example when heading
towards our destination with
those farm animals next to
the stripclub next to the pub
next to the motel next to the
ice cream stand next to the y
& the cathedral on the corner
before you cross that massive
industrial bridge to get to the
metropolis famous for its arts
& culture & nightlife & recent uptick
of petty crime, suicide & recreational drugs

99

Data:

man gets measured by certain obscure criteria
like birth rate, murder rate, per-capita, housing
market, stock market & consumer confidence

news programs tell us we'll be hurting at the pump

how come never once by spirit,
survival of the fittest, olfactory

senses or those detail-oriented
properties & elements, traits
& characteristics of the season? 1

rain
    fall
        & how the world just becomes
            one those blowing tumbling
            out-of-control umbrellas 2

people start love & war
for some of the most
simple sleazy reasons 3

the anchorwoman points
to a chart showing prisoners
die within 12 weeks of captivity 4

the old bowling alley
turned into a bomb
making factory

while kept the fast
food drive-thrus
& pharmacies

all those stripmalls
is what makes it a
great superpower 5

we learn way too much about ourselves
with all that downtime available

why we look forward
to the sports & weather 6

commercials show 'a life of leisure'
with their very sleek contraptions
& vacations yet people seemed

so much happier before
all these discoveries
& inventions

adolescence/adulthood
the difference between
kites & umbrellas 7

man—people talk all this bull
rain finally falls down
in the mountains 8

generation of cut-off
jeans hightop sneaks
hi-fi *hong kong gardens*
post-vietnam i'll freakin

take anyday over
any bullshit going
down these days 9

everything eventually overlaps
genocide, natural catastrophes
while it all becomes a number 10

if a whole tour bus full of tourists
goes over the cliff did they ever exist?
we know culture sure as heck did. . . 11

clowns
& portosans
delivered to ocean 12

Dem-mock-racy:

1. dictators go on book signing tour

2. serial killers receive donations over social media

3. beyonce "queen bee" rescued after midair malfunction

4. big beautiful bill kills millions and makes billionaires richer

5. man found dead in idaho after setting fire in mountains setting up and shooting volunteer firemen

6. all transported by #1 award-winning container company

TV:

the opening story for the local news
tells you all about how a local
farm reopened in vermont

at the end of the international news
an osprey egg found atop the scottish highlands

& in the middle how all the little people spend their lives
just spewing lies & being petty & mean-spirited & corrupt
& self-interested & starting wars & battles making others suffer

man—you look at how jesus got taken out
with present day cycle of violent primitive
behavioral patterns—who exactly are we
worshiping? might over right? man's cruelty
against man? refer to la rochefoucald's "maxims"
nietzsche, freud's "civilization and its discontents"
bbc news directly from london . . . *newark! newark!*

don't worry about any that bullshit in the middle as simply remember
that farm in vermont & osprey egg overlooking the scottish highlands

Psychological Hx:

1. those who make it a living
to not be particularly honest
and bring the constant drama
beware as will almost always
end up making you feel
a part of their trauma

2. it's a strange and quixotic phenomenon
how the brain will so often parse and process
certain data and experiences and perversely
end up feeling guilty for things which were
so insensitively and barbarically done to us

3. an acquaintance close friend of mine
black guy from the projects once told me
(while always seems the most simple thing
which is the most profound thing) that if you grow
up not trusting your family you pretty much end up
parroting this experience and dynamic as the exact
same thing happens with relationships in society

4. life at times just seems like one of those old time raffles
where you got one of those big milk bottles all filled up
with jellybeans in the drug store window and gotta try
to guess how many are in there and if by some stroke
of luck get the closest keep in your room all during
the school year picking out your favorites and those
not too crazy about just leave leftover getting stale
and rotten somehow having lost interest forgotten

5. going back to your childhood—
what were those first colors of crayons?

the first feel & experience of the sea?
when you first lost your virginity?

not really but maybe having
everything to do with identity

6. going thru different phases
of your life
literally got you hiding
back stage
creeping though that trapdoor
keeping the illusion going

7. did any those ancient gods
ever need male bonding
or did the comedians at the
coliseum just do the trick?
ralph kramden pretty much
returned home every night
in the exact same condition
they say in suburbia it's all
about who hides the secret best
the church & country club & your
local cable station with expectation
& destination to become part of that
"lifestyle" fairytale & grand illusion
to impress the neighbors & repress
all those feelings & emotions while
that dream eventually becomes one
of those surreal silent nightmares full of
strangers with no one ever out on their lawn

8. i question people
who get in touch with
their emotions as wonder
why they were so out of touch
with them for such a long period

9. all those mediocre forms of virtue
and predictable & obvious good
deed doers ironically not so
welcoming and pretty alienating
when offer your experience & wisdom

—even this they do in a herd mentality

10. back then crucifixion was an industry
—well what about all those other poor
people nailed to the cross like out of
order phone booths of clark kents not quite
able to make that spiritual heroic metamorphosis

11. take off on your cheap flight to paris
& don't care if you ever make it back
got yourself covered for montmartre
(brie, baguette) the south of france
& if decide to cross the border
where the italian railworkers
are always on strike . . .

the misty island of sicily
coming in on morning ferry

12. you find yourself masturbating
to one of those old black & white
philosophical docs about existentialism
& absurdism & life & death & one of
those sexless female scholars who
happens to speak too about camus
& sartre & being no true answers

13. we are merely just apart of our sum

14. punch a hole through wall
—she sticks her toe through

making you laugh once more
and they say women can't cure . . .

15. once at last you're finally
able to take your own advice
you're on the righteous path
to finding truth & wisdom

16. it will all come around full circle
the paw paw tree will fully grow
& mature & bear those ripe
plump fruits & the clash still
going at it with *armagideon time*

all real wars start with women
fighting at the postcard carousel . . .

Menu:

on my deathbed
it's imperative
they read
wittgenstein's

tractatus philosophicus
passages from proust's
remembrances of things past

then bring in the vaudeville act
mafioso going at the cold cuts
& rabbi with the pirate patch

for that last supper
why not just make it
sweet & sour shrimp

fried chicken wings
& a jug of manischewitz
from *shapiro's* on orchard

when they find you you'll simply
be all coiled in the fetal position
with a grin & do not disturb sign
snooze going off to oldie's radio

100

why is there always this obligatory
ritual & custom where neighbors
feel the compulsion to invite you
over to barbecue to prove you
got social skills & can mix &
mingle to get to know you
better & just feel so much
more uncomfortable in
your own skin awkwardly
standing there forced to have
to discuss matters with people
you got absolutely no respect
for or anything in common with
(life insurance agents & men who
work for the water company talking
about these "swales" in your backyard
& still don't know what the hell they are)
& just want to runaway with your
burger & brew & creep back
across your lawn through
your screen door back
to where it all began

101

in the end you become something
of a squishy tuna fish sandwich
mug of light beer with ice in it
keeping an eye out on the weather
and world affairs—spring comes
late out here to the mountains some
where around mid-april as you start
to plan those projects of repainting
your porch planting a couple more
honey crisp apple and bartlett pear

a bit later on blushing wild apples
blow off autumnal trees tumbling
down the rainy gutter of the steep
hill in the fermenting breeze past
popsicle stick silhouetted steeples
and chimneys of the town finally
settling down secretly tucked
into the sacred sopping ground
having developed a life of their
own where the glowing school
children start their day crashing
through those piping pavlovian
doors picking up their free sticky
cinnamon buns from the bakery
then playfully dancing & leaping
off to elementary—the day ends
where that demented kid goes
through his everyday rituals
& routines as a crossing guard
then shuffles home with stop
sign by his side; all these fine
creatures thriving with a deep
sense of being and belonging
while what else can you really
ask for in this thing called life

OTHER BOOKS BY JOSEPH D. REICH

If I Told You To Jump Off The Brooklyn Bridge (Flutter Press)

A Different Sort of Distance (Skive Magazine Press)

Pain Diary: Working Methadone & The Life & Times Of The Man Sawed In Half (Brick Road Poetry Press)

Drugstore Sushi (Thunderclap Press)

The Derivation Of Cowboys & Indians (Fomite Press)

The Housing Market: a comfortable place to jump off the end of the world (Fomite Press)

The Hole That Runs Through Utopia (Fomite Press)

Taking The Fifth And Running With It: a psychological guide for the hard of hearing and blind (Broadstone Books)

The Hospitality Business (Valeviel Press)

Connecting The Dots To Shangrila: A Postmodern Cultural Hx Of America (Fomite Press)

A Case Study Of Werewolves (Fomite Press)

The Rituals Of Mummification (Sagging Meniscus Press)

Magritte's Missing Murals: Insomniac Episodes (Sagging Meniscus Press)

How To Shoot A Tourist (with a bow & arrow) In A Hot-Air Balloon (Sagging Meniscus Press)

How To Order Chinese During A Hostage Crisis: Dialects, Existential Essays, A Play, And Other Poems (Hog Press)

American Existentialism (Tuba Press)

An Eccentric Urban Guide To Surviving (Analog Submission Press)

The American Book Of The Dead (Xi Draconis Books)

From Premonition To Prophecy (Delinkwent Scholar Press)

Statutes Of David (Pen & Anvil Press)

Aphoristic Variations: a trilogy (Makeshift Press)

I Know Why Old Men Sit In Front Of Windows All Day Sighing & Crying & Living & Dying When The Sun Goes Down On The City At Night (Kung-Fu Treachery Press)

A Case Study Of The Amerikan Dream: the secret life of lounge singers (gnOme books)

Pickles & Provolone & A Friend To Call Your Own (Delinkwent Scholar Press)

A Mom & Son Memoir/Manual On How To Petsit & Take Care Of Domestic Animals (Delinkwent Scholar Press)

Social Studies: a surreal slide presentation of american hx (Audience Askew Press)